TRADING HABITS THAT HURT
FOR HABITS THAT HEAL

Trading Habits that Hurt for Habits that Heal

Carl Dreizler

Servant Publications
Ann Arbor, Michigan

Unless otherwise noted, all passages of Scripture used in this book
are taken from *The New International Version*. Copyright © 1973, 1978,
1983 International Bible Society. Used by permission of Zondervan
Bible Publishers.

Vine Books is an imprint of Servant Publications especially
designed to serve Evangelical Christians.

Published by Servant Publications
P.O. Box 8617
Ann Arbor, Michigan 48107

Cover design by Michael Andaloro
Text design by K. Kelly Nelson

92 93 94 95 96 10 9 8 7 6 5 4 3 2 1

Printed in the United States of America
ISBN 0-89283-788-8

Library of Congress Cataloging-in-Publication Data

Dreizler, Carl, 1954–
     Trading habits that hurt for habits that heal / Carl Dreizler.
          p. cm.
     ISBN 0-89283-788-8
     1. Christian life—1960– . 2. Habit breaking—Religious
aspects —Christianity.   I. Title.
     BV4501.2.D685   1992
     241'.4—dc20   92–452

To my pal, Doug Kyle.

Your friendship has been one of the healing habits of my life.
Whether I think of the days when we first met on Mount Zion,
or the laughter at our weekly lunches over Swiss Chinese food
or the warmth I feel around your dinner table with Cindy and the kids,
I realize what a lucky man I am to call you my friend.

Contents

Acknowledgments

THERE HAVE BEEN so many people who have taken part in this book with me. Close friends have contributed to my own journey of trading habits that hurt for habits that heal. As I started to list all of my close friends and what they've done for me, I filled pages with acknowledgments of thanks. So, although there isn't room to name each person here, I do wish to express my deep love for each of them. When I look at my friendships I realize how truly blessed I am.

I give a very special thank you to Beth Feia and Ann Spangler of Servant Publications for giving me the opportunity to write this book. We've come such a long way from the original idea to the final manuscript. Your talents, insights, and wisdom have been a great help to me. I feel like we've become new friends in the process.

For very special friends like Jan Chantland and Susan La-Flamme, I give thanks and praise God. Your ideas are incorporated within these pages, and your ongoing support is close to my heart.

In thinking back to the days when this book was just an idea, I have fond memories of sitting on my dad's porch with my friend Bill Deist and across the lunch table each week with Doug Kyle. Thanks especially to the two of you when it came time for tossing around so many ideas. Your prayers and the prayers of others have been deeply felt and appreciated.

And last but not least, I thank my parents and siblings for being there as I grew up. I've benefited so much from your love.

Lessons from a Stuck Friend

✳ ✳ ✳

WHEN I WAS A LITTLE BOY I loved to hear the stories of Winnie-the-Pooh. In one particular tale Pooh went to visit his friend Rabbit. After enjoying a snack of honey and condensed milk, Pooh insisted it was time for him to leave.

"Must you?" asked Rabbit politely.

"Well," said Pooh, "I could stay a little longer if it—if you—" and he tried very hard to look in the direction of the larder.

"As a matter of fact," said Rabbit, "I was going out myself directly."

"Oh, well, then, I'll be going on. Good-bye."

"Well, good-bye, if you're sure you won't have any more."

"Is there any more?" asked Pooh quickly.

Rabbit took the covers off the dishes, and said no, there wasn't.

"I thought not," said Pooh, nodding to himself. "Well, good-bye. I must be going on."

So he started to climb out of the hole. He pulled with

his front paws, and pushed with his back paws, and in a little while his nose was out in the open again... and then his ears ... and then his front paws... and then his shoulders... and then—

"Oh help!" said Pooh. "I'd better go back."

"Oh bother!" said Pooh. "I shall have to go on."

"I can't do either!" said Pooh. "Oh, help and bother!"

Now by this time Rabbit wanted to go for a walk too, and finding the front door full, he went out by the back door, and came round to Pooh, and looked at him.

"Hallo, are you stuck?" he asked.

"N-no," said Pooh carelessly. "Just resting and thinking and humming to myself."

"Here, give us a paw."

Pooh Bear stretched out a paw, and Rabbit pulled and pulled and pulled....

"Ow!" cried Pooh. "You're hurting!"

"The fact is," said Rabbit, "you're stuck."[1]

I find much wisdom in this tale, for like Pooh, we as Christians get stuck. Rather than moving on in our relationship with God, we fill our lives with things that keep us in the same place spiritually. Pooh had too much honey and milk. But we get stuck because of the bad habits we've developed through the years: habits that hurt us personally, habits that hurt those around us, and habits that hurt our relationship with God.

For some, a conversion experience with Christ is so transforming that the chains of habits are broken immediately. Most of us, however, must go through a process to change our old patterns. The concept of habit itself does not always need to present a negative picture. For just as we can establish habits that hurt we can establish habits that heal. That's what this book is all about.

In the following chapters we will be looking at seven of the most common habits that keep us stuck and prevent us from growing: doubt, the inability to accept grace, an unforgiving heart, self-hate, dependencies, a lack of integrity, and a lack of spiritual discipline. We'll discuss some alternate habits, antidotes that lead to healing and spiritual growth. Each chapter ends with a few steps to help you create a plan for change in your own life.

If we read more of Pooh's story, we can learn some lessons about getting unstuck. First, gaining freedom takes time. Pooh's friend Christopher Robin told him that he needed to stay in Rabbit's doorway for about a week—until he lost enough weight. He had to learn humility. After all, his friend Rabbit used his feet as a towel rack during the time he was stuck. Pooh went without meals: he had to refrain from the very thing that got him stuck in the first place. Christopher Robin read to Pooh from, as Pooh suggested, "A Sustaining Book such as would help and comfort a Wedged Bear in Great Tightness." Finally, Pooh had friends to help him. When the time came, they all gathered round and pulled together to free their friend.

We too must give ourselves time for change to take place and be willing to face a few lessons of humility in the process. And although you need not go for a week without food as did Pooh, you will have to give up some habits that hurt. Finally, much of the healing will come by reading and hearing God's word and with the support of others who care.

As you begin this book and press on to change habits that hurt into habits that heal, pray for strength. Then consider inviting a friend or two to join you. Perhaps with God's help and the help of others you too will end up like Pooh—unstuck and free!

ONE

Can You Still See Me through the Clouds, God?

* * *

Emerging from the Darkness of Doubt

… But let him ask in faith without any doubting, for the one who doubts is like the surf of the sea driven and tossed by the wind. **Jas 1:6 NAS**

Habits that Hurt

Doubting the promises of God
Giving up in the face of trials
Ignoring God's power
Failing to wait on God's timing

Symptoms

Apathy
Despair
Faithlessness
Impatience

Habits that Heal

Persevering through difficult times
Remembering past blessings
Trusting God's promises

* * *

BEFORE GOD CREATED THE UNIVERSE, only darkness existed. In much the same way, this is how we begin our spiritual lives. Void of a relationship with Christ, we walk through life in a state of spiritual darkness. We are empty inside and unable to see the God of the heavens. Darkness. Void. Night.

Then we discover the truth, the light dawns, and we make a decision to accept the Son of God into our lives. Just as the dawn creeps over the horizon, the Son of God enters our souls and the darkness fades. The world seems brand new. Light. Life. Hope.

Even when a few clouds hinder our view, we know the sun is still there. We can feel it. But when the clouds get thicker and grayer, we long for that experience we felt when dawn came and the darkness left. Deep inside we know the Son of God is still there, but the clouds have blocked our view. Doubt. Fear. Uncertainty.

We long so much to see the sun again, and so we struggle to find it. We begin a journey up the mountain, hoping that the summit will reach above the clouds. The path is narrow and steep. Many times we want to turn back and just live in the clouds. The struggles seem unbearable. But we move on. Leaving the clouds behind, we reach new heights. Life takes on a new meaning. The daylight seems brighter than ever, and the sun much nearer. Promises. Patience. Perseverance.

Finally, the time comes that we must move off the mountaintop and descend back into the clouds. But this time something is different. For even as the clouds surround us we feel the warmth of the sun on our back. And the Son of God seems nearer still. Somehow we know that even the dark clouds will never separate us from the light of life. Maturity. Trust. Faith.

UNBELIEF AND FAITH

No two people would describe their journey of faith in the same way. Yet it seems many of us go through days, months, even years of intermittent clouds. These are times when we're not sure of God's presence and care. The "mountaintop" experiences give us clarity and, if we remember them, can give us strength for the cloudy days. Most of us seek a mature faith in God that trusts even though the storms of life threaten us. Habitual doubt hurts us. Trust is a habit that heals.

Later in this chapter we will look at some of the clouds that come into our lives and threaten our growing faith. But first, let's talk about faith itself. We begin our spiritual lives in a state of darkness or unbelief. Few people miraculously turn from complete darkness to absolute faith without a struggle. Many Christians swing between unbelief and belief, never quite reaching the point of complete faith in God.

Vince is a good example. He was a prosperous fisherman who sold to fine restaurants along the West Coast. Then one of his boats caught fire in a freak accident, cutting his productivity by a third. Soon afterwards an oil spill off the coast caused great loss of sea life, including some of the fish important to Vince's business. One of his children was hospitalized for several weeks. And on top of everything, the stress of these events was causing his marriage to suffer.

Vince had been a Christian for only two years. His walk with Christ had been somewhat difficult up to this point already because of his "I-need-to-see-it-in-order-to-believe-it" approach to life. Vince wanted to believe in Jesus Christ as his personal Savior, but he wanted some guarantee, some proof that God *really* cared for him and that he was concerned about his business and family. Now he really began to doubt the presence of God in his life.

"I'm just not sure anymore." Vince would think to himself. "I always used to think that God was there to encourage his people. But now it's tough to really believe that he's there."

Understanding the way God works is not easy for most people. His power is so limitless, it's no wonder that our finite minds cannot comprehend him at times. Consider the following attributes of God.

God is ever-present yet hears our individual prayers.
God is so big, yet he was able to come to earth as a little baby.

God is invisible yet we see him through others and creation.

God is so powerful yet he chose to become weak.

God allowed his Son to die in order to bring us life.

Vince didn't believe fish stories. He wanted to see the *real*
proof, to confirm the size of the fish and to confirm the size
of his faith. Can you relate to his struggle? "If God would just
speak to me maybe then I would believe." "If I could just witness the same miracles as the Israelites, perhaps then my
faith would grow strong." Why is it so difficult to believe in
God, to believe that he once came to earth in the form of a
little baby and was crucified on a cross to die for the sins of
all people for all time, to believe that he has the attributes
listed above?

GRACEFUL FAITH

I'm convinced that those who constantly struggle with the
issues of faith are the ones who will someday have the
strongest faith. You are not alone if you face times of unbelief
in your life. Nor are you any less worthy than the person
whose faith is unshakable. God's grace is sufficient for all.

The disciples *themselves* did not understand the incredible
power of Jesus. Twice they had seen him provide food for
great multitudes. Yet shortly afterwards they were in a boat
with Jesus and realized they had forgotten to bring enough
bread. Jesus asks them,

"Why do you discuss the fact that you have no bread? Do
you not yet see or understand? Do you have a hardened
heart? Having eyes, do you not see? And having ears, do
you not hear? And do you not remember, when I broke

the five loaves for the five thousand, how many baskets full of broken pieces you picked up?" They said to him, "Twelve."

"And when I broke the seven for the four thousand, how many large baskets full of broken pieces did you pick up?" And they said to him, "Seven."

And he was saying to them, "Do you not yet understand?"

Mk 8:17-21 NAS

Sometimes Jesus asks us the same question. After a time of great worship with God and blessings, we too look at some "loaf" in our life that isn't quite enough and ask God why he came up short this time. It is usually in times of suffering and despair that our faith is tested the most. This is when we are most vulnerable to slipping back into unbelief and doubt.

It doesn't concern me that most Christians fall short of mature faith, because I know that the grace of God accepts us no matter how many times we fall short. What does concern me is that there are thousands of people walking through office buildings, classrooms, and churches who claim to be growing in their faith. They always know the right thing to say and the right way to act. But do they really believe what they say? Are they constantly seeking a stronger, healthier, mature faith in God? As we move through these pages, ask yourself the following questions.

Do I really believe that Jesus is the Lord of my life?

Do I see myself as worthy of his love rather than worthless?

Do others around me see a man or woman who is filled with hope?

Does my faith remain intact when the dark clouds of trouble surround me?

Do I live my life as though I believe in the Son of God?

If you answered "yes" to all of these questions, you probably have a sustaining faith deeply rooted in the love of God. If you could not confidently answer "yes" to these questions, know that you are not alone.

It has been said that *if we completely understood something, then we wouldn't believe it by faith.* Put another way, Hebrews 11:1 says that "faith is being sure of what we hope for and certain of what we do not see." This is perhaps one of the best definitions of faith found in the New Testament. If you must see things to believe, no wonder you have so much trouble believing. Focus on the Hebrews passage. Someday you too may be able to be sure of what you hope for and certain of things you cannot see.

A LESSON FROM PETER

In Matthew 14:22-33 we see Peter's faith in Jesus tested. Jesus sent the disciples to the other side of the Sea of Galilee, while he went up a mountain alone to pray. It was dark. The sea was very rough, and the boat was being battered as a result of the high waves and shifting winds. I picture the disciples huddled together, already a little scared about the situation. As if the storm were not enough, can you imagine their terror to see a man walking toward them on the water? What fear they must have had: out in the middle of a large lake in nasty weather, with a ghost approaching their small boat.

But then they heard a familiar voice, "Take courage, it is I; do not be afraid" (v. 27 NAS). "Whew!" they must have said to one another, "it's Jesus."

In the books of Mark and John we read that Jesus got into the boat with the disciples. But Matthew tells us that something happened before Jesus entered the boat with them. Peter, upon realizing that it was Jesus walking toward them, asked if he too could walk on the water. Everything was going fine for Peter as he took his first few steps toward our Lord. But then the wind came up, and Peter took his focus off of Jesus and back on his fear of the storm. With this he began to sink. Jesus was there to rescue him. Yet he said to Peter (and probably to all the disciples in the boat), "O you of little faith, why did you doubt?" And the wind stopped.

This is perhaps the best illustration for us who struggle with our faith during stormy times. Most of us probably have one foot in the water but are still hanging on to the side of the boat for safety. Think of a time in your life when the waves have frightened you. Perhaps it was the wave of a painful divorce, the wave of losing a child, or the wave of emotional collapse for reasons you didn't understand. Maybe the waves are surrounding the boat you're in right now. During these times it is difficult to trust that the Lord will not let you drown. We must learn from Peter that Jesus will always be there to reach out his hand and save us from the sea of despair.

In Mark 4:35-41 the disciples again were in a boat on the Sea of Galilee. Again a storm came upon them. Mark 4:37, says that "the waves were breaking over the boat so much that the boat was already filling up." But something is different about this story. Jesus was in the boat with them.

We can again apply this situation to our own lives. Sometimes we are hit with rough waters when Jesus is right at our side. Even when we are living wholesome lives focused on Christ and are feeling very good about our spiritual health, tough things can happen to us. Even when we do our best, God does not guarantee us a life without pain. In some cases God actually leads us to rough waters just so we can find even smoother seas later.

How many times have you found yourself in a tough situation, knowing that you were surrounded by the love of Christ and yet responding like the disciples, "Lord, do you not care that I am perishing?" His response is the same to us as it was to them. "Hush. Be still." We must remember in the tough times of life that God *sometimes* allows the storms to overwhelm us. And he *always* uses the storms to help us grow.

WHEN THE CLOUDS GET IN THE WAY

There are so many things that get in the way of our faith. Clouds come out of nowhere to block our spiritual view. We face the pain of broken relationships, poor health, the death of loved ones, financial disaster, and dozens of other hardships. Let's turn now to some of the more general clouds that enter into our lives as Christians.

When God's will doesn't match our will. So often we think we know as much about what is planned for our lives as does God. When I left my job at the age of thirty to attend seminary, I did so because I felt the Lord's call to ministry. I didn't hear a voice from heaven, I just sensed that I was being led in that direction. Having a background in business administration, I attended seminary with the goal of serving as executive pastor in a local church. I was so convinced that I was headed for such a full-time ministry in the church, I actually believed that it was God's will too.

Shortly after graduating from seminary, I began searching for the type of position I had in mind. I discovered that while there were a great number of churches who could have used an executive pastor for overseeing the facilities, staff, and finances of the church, not many were looking for such a person. I became very confused about God's will for my future.

The months of unemployment and searching presented to me the toughest part of my journey toward a lasting faith. The circumstances don't seem as devastating in hindsight. But when I was in the midst of them, the darkness overshadowed me. The underlying struggles were the questions I was asking about God. Where did he go? With all the academic material I learned in seminary, why did I feel further from God than ever? Why is life so painful? When will the issues in my life be resolved? Do I even believe in God any more?

Soon different doors began to open up. For a couple of years I worked with over fifty rescue missions around the country, helping them raise funds in order to feed and shelter more of God's hungry and hurting people. It was an experience that changed my life. Then I moved on to a company that provides psychiatric care for Christian people dealing with depression, addictions, suicidal thoughts, and a wide variety of other issues. Again, I grew immensely through this experience. I discovered that ministry is not simply working full-time in a church.

After several years of working in various situations I found that God's will was not necessarily what I *thought* his will would be. What I saw was God closing the door on something *I* felt called to do, when actually God was directing me through another door. Perhaps you have been disappointed at times in your life when an opportunity has not worked out. Yet the alternate road may take you to a place where you never would have otherwise gone.

When circumstances overwhelm us. It's easier to talk about God's will when it comes to things like which job we are to choose. But how do we explain God's will when a child is taken through cancer? Or an earthquake kills hundreds of people?

No analysis can explain with complete clarity why terrible things happen to us. We can say that God allows bad things to happen. We can say that Satan is extremely powerful on earth. We can say that we live in a sinful world. And we can say that all things work together for good. All of these statements are true. Yet they don't ease the pain when tragedies strike. During these times we are particularly vulnerable to our faith shaking.

Catherine Marshall went through such a time. After earnestly praying for her granddaughter, who was born with severe medical problems, the child died. This great woman of God was shattered. Her family and friends surrounded her to provide comfort and suggestions for healing. But this time Catherine just couldn't understand why God didn't answer her prayers. Here are some of her words during the time of her "darkest night."

What is destroying me is that I understand nothing about it, nothing about anything that happened. What's wrong with going all-out for something you believe in? God likes single-eyed people, doesn't he? It says so in Scripture. Well, I've always tried to be one hundred percent in everything I do. And always before, God honored my efforts. Why not this time? Why have I been flattened so completely? I know it's happened to others. Great saints have gone through dark nights a thousand times worse than mine. But they almost seemed to ask for it, seeking some higher plane of spirituality. I didn't ask for anything for myself, only that a tiny baby be healed, and God not only refused that request, but turned his back on me. I don't understand.[1]

Catherine read Isaiah 53, which foretells the suffering of Christ. She read it as she never had before. And she found

some answers by refocusing on the fact that Christ had to suffer a great deal on the cross to complete a plan that was
good. She explains part of her healing process.

> Then came this revelation: when life hands up situations
> we cannot understand, we have one of two choices. We can
> wallow in misery, separated from God. Or we can tell him,
> "I need you and your presence in my life more than I need
> understanding. I choose you, Lord. I trust you to give me
> understanding and an answer to all my Why's?—only if
> and when you choose."[2]

Moses faced some overwhelming circumstances in Numbers 11. The nation of Israel, now free from Pharaoh in Egypt,
was beginning to forget the blessings of that freedom. They
murmured and complained about the bland taste of manna,
the food God had provided. The stress of trying to lead hundreds of thousands of complaining people finally got to
Moses. He cried out to the Lord, "Why have you brought this
trouble on your servant? What have I done to displease you
that you put the burden of all this people on me?" (Num
11:11 NIV).

Moses continued, "I cannot carry all these people by myself; the burden is too heavy for me. If this is how you are
going to treat me, put me to death right now—if I have
found favor in your eyes—and do not let me face my own
ruin" (Num 11:14-15 NIV). Moses, perhaps the greatest man
in the Old Testament, was so troubled with his circumstances
that he cried out for God to take his life. No one is exempt
from facing overwhelming situations.

Many people reach a point sometime during their life
when things don't seem to make sense. For some, a single
traumatic event starts the pain. For others, several stressful
events over a short period of time build up a pressure that

must be released. Often it's a lifetime of problems that finally burst out. Going through hard times is not a pleasant journey, but it's a necessary one, I think. Through it we learn what it's like to need God and to trust God. This can help us move into a relationship of constant companionship with Jesus Christ.

When we move away. Still another time when our faith seems to fade occurs when we move away from our relationship with Christ. Hectic schedules keep us from regular worship of him. If we haven't been reading the Bible regularly, we can lose our Christian perspective on life and start to doubt God. It's good to ask when we are feeling distant from the Lord, "Have I moved away from him?"

The only way to remain strong in our faith, whether life is going well or difficulties face us, is to remain close to God. The times when my knowledge of him and my faith in him have grown most were those times when I was deeply and regularly involved in Bible study and regular praise time. We will talk about some of the spiritual disciplines that help us to do that in this and other chapters of this book.

JAMES AND JOB: MOUNTAIN CLIMBERS

Earlier in this chapter we used the analogy of climbing a mountain to get above the clouds of doubt. The mountain road will almost surely be treacherous, difficult, and narrow, but one who seeks a mature faith is willing to climb it. James tells us,

> Consider it all joy, my brethren, when you encounter various trials, knowing that the testing of your faith produces endurance. And let endurance have its perfect result, that

you may be perfect and complete, lacking in nothing. But if any of you lacks wisdom, let him ask of God, who gives to all men generously and without reproach, and it will be given to him. But let him ask in faith without any doubting, for the one who doubts is like the surf of the sea driven and tossed by the wind.   **Jas 1:2-6 NAS**

These words may seem completely contrary to the way we feel when the trials hit. How often do we consider the toughest times of our life as joyful? How often do we trust in God enough to ask for his help? Consider Moses earlier. Rather than asking for help, he questioned why everything was going so poorly and even wished for his life to end.

But incredibly, good things take place because of trials. Why does this happen? Let's look further at this passage from James.

The testing of your faith produces endurance (1:3). Tough times in life can actually make us stronger, more faithful people. An Olympic gold medalist in figure skating only reaches that point because she fell thousands of times on the hard, cold ice. Each fall taught her something. It is the same with our faith. We learn through our difficulties that God always comes through. And often he has something to teach us about ourselves or about who he is.

Endurance produces its perfect result (1:4). Even though we may not realize it in the midst of the rough seas, hard times produce changes in us. Almost anyone who has been through very painful experiences in their lives can tell you that it was a turning point of one kind or another. Sometimes the pain gets so intense that we are forced to seek the professional help we've needed for years. And very commonly, people on the other side of difficult times are able to show much more compassion toward others who face similar situations in their lives. People who endure become more godly, I'm convinced. And Scripture tells us so.

Let him ask of God, who gives to all men generously (1:5). Difficult times bring us to our knees before God. I keep a daily journal. In times when things seem to be going well in my life, the journal entries are relatively short. During the difficult times, I am able to pour my heart out before God. While some of my entries may be similar to the painful, questioning words of Moses, others have brought me to a new realization of my deep need for God's intervention in various areas of my life.

Just as we take things like our automobiles for granted until they break down, we often take God for granted when everything in our lives is going well. When we break down, we are often forced to come alongside of him and ask for his wisdom in the situation we face.

Let him ask in faith without any doubting (1:6). Not only are we brought closer to God during the trials in our lives, but we are brought face-to-face with our own faith in Christ. This verse seems to complete the circle that began the Scripture passage. When we ask, "How can we possibly be joyful during times of trial?" the answer is that we must remove doubt. For when we doubt we are "like the sea driven and tossed by the wind." Yet when we trust, we can truly have joy in our hearts, even amid the storms.

Everyone going through difficult times should read the book of Job. He provides us with an incredible testimony of endurance and long-suffering. Job had done nothing to deserve the pain and heartache that came his way. He was a man who put his faith in God above all. And when life completely collapsed, Job did the opposite of what most of us would do. Instead of turning from God in rebellion and asking "Why?" he summoned a faith that was stronger still.

STARTING UP THE MOUNTAIN

When the clouds become unbearable, it is difficult for us to start the journey up the mountain. Sometimes we are prompted to begin by a gentle prod from someone who loves us. Some people are led to begin the journey toward a growing faith through their own desire to grow spiritually. Still others are encouraged to start the climb by an event in their lives.

During my tough time of unemployment, instead of becoming more involved in the church, I moved away from God because of the doubt surrounding my circumstances. During this time when I felt separated from him, I had an encounter that helped me take the first steps up the mountain and back to a close relationship with Christ.

It had been a melancholy December day for me. Feelings of emptiness seemed to overshadow the joy of the holiday season. Most of my morning had been spent grieving over six months of unemployment and missing one of my closest friends, who had recently moved away. He had been a great source of encouragement to me.

As I sat in my favorite chair in the beautiful oceanfront home where I was staying, I noticed a young boy writing in the sand below my window. After he walked away I was shocked to read his words, "Satan Rules," followed by a profanity directed at God. I watched as the young man walked down the beach and hacked at a clump of seaweed with his diving knife. His anger became more apparent as he began to throw rocks at the sea gulls.

I reflected back to a time twenty years ago, when I too had walked on a beach to escape the pain of adolescence. As the boy walked into a cove and was lost from my view, I had a mounting concern for him and decided to go down to the beach. I found him at the end of the cove.

The boy's name was Jason. He had been very close to his grandma, and she had recently died. His parents were divorced. His dog had gotten hit by a car. Jason wondered, Does God really care? Why does he let people die? "I don't think God is good at all," he stated.

I ached for this young boy who moments before had been a stranger to me. But could I help him when I felt so inadequate to handle my own pain? I had to try. Suddenly the words seemed to flow from my mouth.

I talked about God's mysterious ways, about Jesus' victory over death, and about heaven, where all pain will finally be erased. I told Jason that Jesus is always with us in our pain. Jason smiled briefly. He seemed so calm now as we both looked out at the sea. I felt compelled to say one more thing.

"Jason, you wrote in the sand about Satan. He would love to see this sadness destroy us. When we're sad and discouraged, Satan has the greatest opportunity to win. But we can stop him. Just remember that God loves you, Jason, and he cares that you hurt. So do I. He even allows you to be angry at him. Just don't give up on his goodness."

As I left I noticed Jason walking back to the letters written in the sand, now partially erased by the rushing waves. I watched him take a stick and scratch out the words he had written only a half hour before. In a short while the tide would come in and make the sand flawless and pure—much as God erases the scratchings of our sin when we go to him and confess.

I sank into my chair again and reflected on what had just

happened. At first I had thought I was there for Jason, but I realized now that God had put Jason there for me. It took a young man, writing in the sand about his anger at God, to free me up to release my anger and doubt. And what I said to Jason about Jesus were the very words I needed to hear myself.

EXAMPLES OF STRONG FAITH

There seem to be a few people around whose faith can withstand the often unbearable trials of life. Even when the chips are down, they have a positive attitude. As opportunities come forth to help the needy, they are often the first to volunteer. They bake meals for the family who is out of work. They always know the right comforting words for someone who is discouraged. Their knowledge of the Scriptures is vast and keen.

I have a grandmother who comes very close to fitting this description. While I'm sure she would say her life has been filled with nothing but joy, I know that she has had to face some very difficult times. She turned ninety just this month, so she can't write like she used to. She would send hundreds and hundreds of cards each year to the people in her life: not just to her kids, grandkids, and great-grandkids, but to the neighbor down the street, to the grocer across the highway, to the pastor of the church, to the fellow parishioner's son who is away on military duty. She prays without ceasing. The pages of her Bible are frayed from years of reading. This incredible woman of faith amazes me.

In Mark 5 there is another great woman of faith. Picture the setting if you can. Hundreds of people were following Jesus as he walked with a man named Jairus, whose daughter was dying. He had asked Jesus to lay his hands upon her and heal her. People were crowded all around this great man who had been going about the countryside teaching and healing people. Everyone wanted to get a glimpse of him.

One woman in the crowd seemed particularly anxious to get to Jesus. Suffering from a hemorrhage that had been with her for twelve years, she knew that finally someone had come who could help her. Perhaps she was thinking, "He will heal me. I know it. I've just got to get close to him. With all of these people, he probably doesn't have time for me. But if I can just brush against him or even touch his clothing, perhaps I can be healed of this pain." No one really noticed as she reached between people in the crowd and for a moment touched the robe of Jesus. No one, that is, except Jesus himself.

Suddenly the momentum of the group stopped. Jesus turned and looked behind him. Hundreds of faces were looking at him, perhaps puzzled because he had stopped. And he asked, as he surveyed the masses, "Who touched my garment?"

The disciples found the question somewhat preposterous, as dozens of people had touched him in the last moment alone. But the woman, now healed of her pain, fell down before the Lord. The noise of the crowd died as the woman began to speak, trembling with both fear and the excitement of being healed. She told Jesus that all she had wanted was to get near him. And before all the people she told how her affliction had gone away the moment she touched the hem of his garment. "You have made me well, Teacher." Jesus said to the woman, "Daughter, it is your faith that has made you well."

Think about this woman next time you go to the Lord. Are you reaching for him with all of your heart because you sincerely believe that he can make miracles happen? Your faith can make you well too. And it can help you climb mountains.

Our faith is not only important in *our* walk with God, but our faith can actually bring help to a loved one who is hurting. A centurion came to Jesus and told him about the great pain of his paralyzed servant. And because of the strong belief of the centurion, Jesus healed the servant without even going to him (see Mt 8:5-13). As you work on building your faith, remember that you can use such belief not only for yourself, but for others. In the meantime, see if you can find someone whose faith is strong to intercede for you.

FOCUS ON FAITH

There are at least two ways we can grow in our faith. One is to experience the challenges of life and to learn to trust in God through them. The other is to turn to Scripture and learn from the words and illustrations God gives us. In fact, the more time we spend learning from the latter, the better prepared we will be to learn from the former. And it's less painful.

Everyone's journey of faith is unique. Your faith will be challenged and will grow through different circumstances than the ones I've faced. And so will the faith of your parents, children, spouse, and friends. But let's consider some lessons from the Scriptures to help us on our journey toward a stronger faith in God.

Step One: Evaluate your commitment. Are you sure about your faith? Have you asked Jesus Christ to become the master of your life? If you have, he's there. There is no need to ask him again. When Jesus says in Revelation 3:20, "Behold, I stand at the door and knock. If any one answers I will come in," he is not stopping by for a quick cup of coffee. He is there to stay.

For many, belief in God is such a struggle. Every time

there is an altar call these people go forward, each time hoping that this profession of faith will be the one that makes them "feel" spiritual. Once we are saved, we need not come forward each time—unless, of course, it is to *reaffirm* our faith in Christ. When Jesus washed the disciples' feet, Peter asked that his hands, feet, and head be washed as well. Jesus replied, "A person who has had a bath needs only to wash his feet; his whole body is clean" (Jn 13:10). Similarly, once we ask Christ into our life we have washed away the sins of the old person. We need only "foot washings" to receive forgiveness for our everyday sins.

Find comfort in the fact that once you have asked Jesus Christ to be your personal Savior, you are a child of his forever. Even if you don't *feel* any different at first, God will begin a good work in your life. Take a few minutes to write a one or two-page personal assessment entitled "Where I Am in My Christian Faith." Consider writing a paragraph or two about each of the following questions.

1. How do I feel about my relationship with Jesus Christ?
2. In what ways has my faith grown over the past few months?
3. Where are the voids in my spiritual walk?
4. What changes do I need to make to help my faith grow?

Hopefully this will help you discover whether or not you have made that initial commitment to Christ and where you are with God right now. I encourage people to write one of these personal reviews at least once a quarter. I promise you that no two reports will be the same.

Step Two: Focus on the Lord Jesus. We again look at Peter's lesson on faith. Remember how well he was doing walking on the water? Things seemed all right while he was focused upon

Jesus who was walking with him. But as soon as Peter turned away from the Lord and saw the howling wind and rushing waves, he took his focus off of Jesus and gave in to his fear.

Throughout this book there are many suggestions of ways you can keep your eyes focused on Jesus. See especially the final chapter regarding spiritual disciplines. For the time being, think of three things to do regularly with the Lord that you are not doing now. For example, attend a midweek Bible study, begin keeping a prayer journal, or spend five minutes a day with God.

Step Three: Remember the blessings of the past. Like the Israelites who had received manna and quail in the desert, like the disciples who had seen Jesus feed thousands, how quickly we forget the miracles and blessings God has given us. Take a moment to list five of the blessings or even miracles he has brought to your life. Keep an ongoing list so that you can refer to your past blessings whenever things look discouraging.

Blessings from God to Me

1. _____
2. _____
3. _____
4. _____
5. _____

Step Four: Give God the problem. If your faith is faltering because there are problems overwhelming you, turn to Jesus for help. Don't allow yourself to think that problems only come to people who do not have favor in God's eyes. Remember righteous Job?

Like the woman with the hemorrhage, bring your issues to Jesus. Write down the things that you need to bring to him right now.

Problems for God

1. _____
2. _____
3. _____
4. _____
5. _____

Perhaps your faith is so weak you have trouble coming to the Lord. Find a spiritual mentor. Think of someone you know who seems to have strong faith, and ask him or her to pray with you and for you. That person can be the centurion in your life who intercedes for you. Your faith can grow through the strong faith of another.

Step Five: Ask God for his grace to help you believe in his promises. God has promised to always be with us. He promised the people of Israel that he would see them through to the Promised Land. Jesus promises to be with us "even to the end of the age" (Mt 28:20). We don't know what he has planned—for our relationships, for our time, or for our careers. Strong faith enables us to accept whatever he has planned.

A mature faith in God does not come easily. Make a commitment to pray regularly that his grace will lead you to a stronger relationship with him. You cannot build a stronger faith alone. You will need his help; and it's there for the taking.

An article in *Life* magazine asked people to describe how they view God. Cody Faircloth, who is seventy, and his sixty-seven-year-old wife Martha Nell raise cattle, hogs, chickens, and milk cows, as well as grow corn and oats on their farm in Florida. Part of Cody's response regarding God follows.

You have to understand where God is coming from. You don't blame God for dry weather. You adjust. We know we won't have as much corn for feed, so we'll sell off more stock. So we get a low price. Next year it'll go back up. God is merciful. I don't think paradise is here. But I do believe we were put here for our enjoyment. We enjoy every day of it.

God is so close to me, whatever I'm doing. He's with us while we crush the corn, bale the hay, and gather the oats growed on our place. From here I can look at the old house and see my mother's rosebushes. She's gone, but the roses keep right on blooming. That's how it is with God. He's here now and will be when we're gone. He'll just go on and on, blooming right along, like them roses.[3]

The passage we studied from the book of James talks about our being made perfect through endurance. God's promises are true. Ask that his will be done in your life, no matter what it may be. If "the weather is dry," or your faith seems weak, pray to God regularly. For while men and women forget about promises, God will never let us down. The roses keep blooming. That is the very essence of faith.

We may not have the risen Christ before us as the disciple Thomas did. We may not be able to put our hands in his side or feel the nail-holes in his hands. But the ancient words God gave to Jacob are with us today:

I will be with you and protect you wherever you go.... I will not leave you until I have done all that I promised you.

Gn 28:15

TWO

Why Take the Elevator When I Can Climb the Stairs?

* * *

Working to Be Saved in Spite of God's Grace

For by grace you have been saved through faith;
and that not of yourselves, it is the gift of God;
not as a result of works, that no one should boast.

Eph 2:8-9 NAS

Habits that Hurt

Working for God's acceptance
Misunderstanding God's grace
Feeling unworthy of God's love

Symptoms

Spiritual workaholism
Approval-seeking
People-pleasing

Habits that Heal

Accepting God's grace as a free gift
Responding with obedience
Doing good works *because* we are saved

* * *

EUGENE O'NEIL SAID, *"Man is born broken. He lives by mending. The grace of God is glue."* Grace is the very best prescription for turning habits that hurt into habits that heal. It is the glue that allows us to fall short without our whole Christian life breaking apart. When you fail to meet some of the goals you set in this book, Christ's grace will be sufficient for you. When you disobey the laws given in Scripture, his grace will abound. When you feel dirty because you fall into moral failure, Jesus' grace will wash you white as snow.

Grace saturates every part of our relationship with God. Jesus came to the earth through grace. He died for our sins by grace. We will enter his kingdom because of grace. We have been made holy by grace. And he loves us unconditionally by grace.

GLIMPSES OF GRACE

One night a close friend and I were driving to San Diego to watch our favorite team, the Los Angeles Dodgers, play at Jack Murphy Stadium. During the hour or so drive, we began a discussion regarding God's gift of free grace. The conversation revolved around the difficulty many of us have in understanding and accepting this gift. I was seeking some everyday ideas to illustrate how we can reflect God's grace in a human way to one another.

We arrived at the stadium hoping to purchase two seats at the regular price. As we walked from our car trying to decide what our best move would be, a man asked us if we needed tickets. He had some extras given to him that he wasn't going to use. What's more, the man said we could just take his extras free of charge. Much to our excitement, the tickets put us on the field level near the Dodger dugout. As we sat down just in time for the first pitch, my friend looked at me and said, "I think you just received a simple example of what the free gift of grace is like."

Although a couple of baseball tickets are a far cry from the incredible gift of God's grace, this illustration somewhat parallels how we receive this treasure. The world would say that we should have to pay for our tickets into the game. At least we should have worked for them in some way. Perhaps we should have at least bought a hot dog for the man who gave them to us. But they were free! My friend and I didn't do anything to *deserve* the free tickets.

God's grace is bestowed upon us in spite of our not deserving it. In fact, he bestows it even though we're very *undeserving*. It has been given freely *despite* our sinful nature. We can't buy our way into his kingdom, nor do we have to earn our way into his kingdom. In fact, unlike entry to Jack Murphy Stadium in San Diego, with God we don't even need a ticket. The gates are wide open to all who believe.

Though the grace shown to us by fellow believers is not of the same magnitude as the grace given by Christ, it can help us view this miraculous undeserved gift of favor. As I look back, there were several examples of grace shown to me during the difficult time of my unemployment.

I have a wonderful mechanic who comes right to my home or place of business to work on the car. During this tough time in my life he spent several hours changing the oil, giving a tune-up, and checking for other service needs. When the work was completed, I got out my checkbook. Knowing that I was unemployed, he said, "No charge." I insisted that he at least let me pay for the parts. But he refused. This man drove for more than an hour to get to my house (on the Southern California freeways no less), spent a few hours of his time, replaced parts that cost him money, and then drove another hour or so to get home. Yet there was no charge for his service. That's grace.

Although I was far from poverty, it was a pretty discouraging time. One day there was a plain white envelope in my mailbox. Inside was a one hundred dollar bill folded inside a blank sheet of paper. To this day I don't know who sent it to me. A free gift from someone unseen: that's grace.

When the news came that I finally got an interview for a wonderful job, one friend gave me a check and said, "Thought you might need a new pair of shoes for your interview." At the same time he forgave a debt I owed him. That's grace.

UNDERSTANDING GOD'S GRACE

Do you ever wonder if God gets frustrated with us? If he does, I'm sure one of the things he gets most frustrated with is our inability to understand and accept the gift of grace. I can just imagine what he'd say if he were trying to tell us in simple language. "Okay, listen. You don't have to do a thing to be saved. You don't have to work. You don't have to go to church every Sunday. You don't have to smile all the time. You don't have to get straight A's on your exams. You don't have to feel guilty when you say no to some commitment at church. You don't really have to understand completely what grace is. You don't even have to empty your pockets when the offering plate is passed around. All you have to do is have faith in me—that's it."

We've always heard, "There's no such thing as a free lunch." When we're offered a free gift through some tele-marketing call or some direct mail piece, our first response is, "What's the catch? How long do I have to sit through a semi-nar to receive this gift? What resort is trying to sell time shares now?" There's got to be a catch to any offer for a free gift—right? Wrong. Grace is given by God absolutely free. No seminars to hear. No time share to visit. It's yours. Right now. Today. Forever.

In high school Barry just had to be on the honor roll every quarter. In his business career he wanted his supervisor to mark the category of "outstanding" in describing every qual-ity listed in his annual review. When making sales presenta-tions, he based his effectiveness on the number of positive comments he heard from his peers during that particular week. He wanted people to say, "Good job, Barry" so he always tried to work especially hard. When he fell short, he took it pretty hard.

For many years, Barry did the same thing spiritually. Every time sin crept into his life, each day he slept in rather than attending church, whenever he said something that hurt another person, he felt that he had let God down. "I didn't perform up to his standards," Barry would say to himself. So he tried harder the next week to earn God's approval.

Barry represents a lot of Christians who seek approval and acceptance from God by doing more things to please him. But once we learn what a special gift God's grace is, we don't have to perform to gain his acceptance. We want to be men and women after the heart of God, but when we fall short, we realize that God still loves us. And when we really blow it, we no longer think of something to do that is especially spiritual to make up for it. Paul tells us in Romans 5:20 that "where sin increased, grace abounded all the more."

So if grace expands beyond our sin, what's to keep us from sinning as much as we want? A relationship of deep love and respect. Allow me to draw an illustration from my childhood. When I was a little boy, milk was still being delivered to the front door in half-gallon glass bottles. I remember one day trying to get some milk from the top shelf of the refrigerator. I had to stand on a chair to reach the top shelf. To my surprise, the full bottle was too heavy for me to handle. As it hit the kitchen floor, shattered glass and milk went everywhere.

Afraid I might be punished, I scampered quickly up to my bedroom. Secretly I hoped that my parents would think that one of my siblings caused the mess. But they knew better. And they didn't punish me. In fact, they came to my room, hugged me, and asked if I was okay. Something changed that day. I saw my parents as people who cared more about my well-being than they did about my mistakes. It made me want to obey them all the more as I grew into adolescence.

And so it is in our relationship with God. Once we realize

what a treasure we have in the gift of grace and a relationship with the Father, we seek to do as he would want us to do. We develop a sense of trust that restrains us from actively rebelling.

If you are a spiritual high achiever who tries to gain God's attention, take a break. You have nothing to prove to him. He cares more about your well-being than your mistakes. His grace has been given to you, absolutely free.

A THREE-STEP PROGRAM FOR UNDERSTANDING GOD'S GRACE

First we must completely remove ourselves from worldly explanations. Grace cannot be understood in a world that requires performance for a reward. The examples of human grace given so far can help understand the concept, but they do not do justice to the grace God gives to us.

Assume you are a missionary in the deepest jungles of a foreign country. Your work has developed quite a following of believers. Suddenly one night the people turn against you. They burn your hut and then kill your spouse and children.

Immediate transportation is sent to return you safely home, but you decide to stay. Alone you rebuild a home for yourself. You not only forgive your attackers, you find ways to help them, comfort them, and provide new medicines for healing their sickness.

Not many of us would be able to help those who had destroyed our home, killed our children, and turned us away. This is why grace is so difficult to grasp. For although we couldn't do these things, God does them for us every day. We turn from him, destroy what he created, and ignore his Son. He offers us peace, love, grace.

God's grace is a completely free and glorious gift, unlike any favor ever done for us or any material gift ever received. Since it's not rational to man, we have to temporarily sever the logical thought processes we use to prove and comprehend things.

Secondly, we must realize how badly we need grace. We must remember how much God has forgiven since the beginning of time and in our own lives. What would our sentence be if we had to go before a spiritual judge with our sin, as a criminal goes before a jury?

A current philosophy in our culture urges us to find the meaning of life within ourselves. But to understand grace we must see the void within and depend on God to fill it.

Our society also keeps us from seeing our need for grace by its emphasis on achievement as a source of worth. We easily develop the notion that we gain God's approval also through our work. Churches reinforce this idea when they teach that the Christian life is adhering to rules and standards of behavior.

Thirdly, we must understand the magnitude of the sacrifice of Christ on the cross. Separated from God we are the guilty and sinful people discussed in the last point. But through the death of Jesus on the cross, we have been set free from guilt and sin. He accepts us just as we are and has made us righteous. The theological term for this act of God is *justification* or "to put in the right."

Not only have we been made righteous through the sacrifice of Jesus, we are also made holy. This is known as *sanctification*. We can find this no other place than in Christ who lives through us. Hebrews 10:10 says, "And by that will, we have been made holy through the sacrifice of the body of Jesus Christ once for all."

This saving act is even more magnificent when we think of

who God is. He is not simply "the great man in the sky," he is totally "other," with attributes far beyond anything we could be. He knows everything there is to know about the universe. He is everywhere in the universe at the same time. He created everything we see around us. He can part the Red Sea, turn water into wine, make the blind see, raise the dead, bring forth a child from a virgin woman. Yet this mighty God humbled himself for us. He made the ultimate sacrifice of his Son for our sakes.

WHAT GOOD IS GRACE?

The sixth chapter of Romans explains that we are no longer under the control of sin, once we have come into a relationship with the crucified and risen Christ. Sin is no longer our master; nor is the law, nor is condemnation. All of these things have been put behind us and replaced with grace. Romans 6:14 says, "For sin shall not be master over you, for you are not under law, but under grace."

Since we are no longer under the law, does that give us leeway to be disobedient? Of course not. Hebrews 12:14 instructs us to "strive for holiness." Grace is what empowers us in a life of obedience to God's commandments and living for his glory.

According to Acts 18:27, grace also helps us to believe. On the one hand, grace enables us to believe; on the other, belief enables us to receive grace. This is one of the mysteries of the Christian faith.

The breadth of the grace of God is beyond our understanding. But despite its mystery, let's list a few of the key phrases that describe grace so that we can review them regularly.

Grace...

- has saved us through faith
- is the basis of our relationship with God
- is undeserved
- is given freely
- cannot be repaid
- sets guilty sinners free from judgment
- has given us the kingdom of God
- helps us obey God's word
- assists us in facing tough times
- declares us righteous before God
- declares us holy before God
- causes us to be humble before him
- helps us to accept God's forgiveness
- allows us to forgive others when it makes no sense to
- rids us of "ought's," "should's," "must's," "do's," and "don'ts"
- replaces feelings of failure with a positive self-worth
- frees us from guilt
- provides us with all the approval we'll ever need
- frees us from the chains of the past
- allows us to show its face to others around us
- lets us accept others as God accepts us.

GRACE AND WORKS

Our human nature tells us what is wrong or right, sometimes without regard to our faith. For example, most people know that killing someone is wrong. But the topic of grace and works is not so black and white. Both are positive parts of the Christian's walk. Some people feel that by working hard they are guaranteed a place at the front of the line when heaven calls. They don't understand that we are saved through our faith by grace alone—not by the works we perform. Works are not a prerequisite to grace, though they do glorify God, are requested by God, and are rewarded by God.

Irene became so obsessed with her work that her emotional and spiritual health were threatened. Now recovering from severe depression and a suicide attempt, Irene went through extensive therapy in order to find the cause of her pain. Irene came to see that she spent virtually every waking hour working. As if raising four children wasn't enough for her to do, she was always doing special favors for her neighbors and for people at church. She felt a responsibility to care for her ailing and aging parents. She cooked meals, wiped runny noses, cleaned houses, ran a car pool, washed clothes, and ran errands. Irene never took time for herself, and she found personal time with God an impossibility.

Satisfying the needs of everyone around her had become a compulsion to Irene. "I must not let others down," she would say. This need to always please everybody is what drove Irene to thoughts of suicide and despair. Because she felt that she could never do enough for anybody, life didn't seem worth living anymore.

Though it would take her a long time to break the old patterns, Irene finally learned that she didn't have to work constantly to gain the approval of her parents, her children, her husband, and others. She now balances her time so that there is something left for her. The biggest lesson Irene learned was the meaning of grace. God loves her for the person she is, not for the duties she performs.

We can learn a lot from Irene's experience. In the home we strive to be a loving mate and to raise our kids to be model citizens. In the corporate world we usually have to work hard and perform well to get the promotion or the raise we want. In the sports world the baseball players who are best at fielding the ball get Golden Glove awards. The best actor or actress receives an Oscar. In school the person who gets the best grades is called the valedictorian. We are a society driven by performance and achievement. Have we succumbed to the world's expectations, or are we content to be the person God has made us?

WHEN WORKS TURN SOUR

Many people in the working world today have fallen into the trap of workaholism, which is considered an addiction by some experts. There are lots of reasons someone may become a workaholic. Some people work hard simply because they want to move up the corporate ladder. Others work hard because they enjoy what they do so much they can never seem to stop. Many workaholics just need something to keep them busy. It helps them avoid pain in their lives or a difficult situation at home. Overwork is quite often a symptom of low self-esteem.

On the surface workaholism may not seem to be harmful to anyone or anything. In fact, many workaholics find their reward in people saying, "Can you believe how hard Dawn works? Her car is here when I arrive in the morning, and it's here when I leave at night. And last Saturday when I came to pick up something, she was here then too! She's really committed to our company." But workaholism can affect our spiritual life and our relationships.

We can also fall into a martyr complex—feeling as though we're the one doing all of the work and no one else is doing their fair share. This thinking is usually counterproductive to our work and to our relationships. Martha, the sister of

Lazarus, is the prime scriptural victim of this syndrome. In the tenth chapter of the Gospel of Luke we find her distracted by all the work of being a good hostess. But she becomes frustrated because her sister Mary is sitting with Jesus rather than helping her in the kitchen. "Lord," she asks, "do you not care that my sister has left me to do all the serving alone?"

Finally, competitiveness can turn hard work sour. There is no shame in trying to be the best at something; people who have excelled deserve to be recognized. The problems come when the one who is best loses his or her integrity, humility, compassion, or focus on God in reaching that goal. Many competitive people will do anything to get promotions, recognition, or acceptance from others.

- Someone drops a bit of negative gossip to the boss regarding a peer who is in line with them for a promotion.
- A teenager is secretly pleased to find out her grade on the final exam was higher than her best friend's.
- The senior pastor's secretary passes off one of her responsibilities to a new member of the clerical staff because she dislikes that part of her job.

It is in these situations and others like them that our works become dishonorable to God and unfair to others.

SPIRITUAL WORKAHOLICS

The major problem we're focusing on here is created when this worldly *"I must work hard to get recognized"* attitude carries over into our spiritual life. Because we are used to the model just described in the physical world, in which good works seem necessary for acceptance, we often transfer these values over to our walk with God. Many Christians are stuck in a cycle of trying to please God through their works—thinking that the harder they work, the more likely it is that they will get God's Golden Glove, his Oscar, his award as valedictorian. But Ephesians 2:8-9 tells us this just isn't so: "For by grace you have been saved through faith; and that not of yourselves, it is the gift of God; not as a result of works, that no one should boast." Works are something we give back because of our award of grace, not something we do to earn it.

A pastor once told me that a member of his elder board came to him and said, "I've been a Christian for over thirty years, and I'm still not sure I deserve to go to heaven. I never feel like I'm doing enough to please God." This man doesn't understand the concept of grace. And unfortunately, there are a lot of people serving coffee on church patios, attending elder meetings, and leading Bible studies because it makes them feel more secure in their salvation.

Many of us unwittingly fall into the trap of working for God's acceptance. We start out serving the Lord in one way or another with very sincere intentions, motivated by the grace and love we experienced in our relationship with God. But soon some other factor takes over. Perhaps the worldly patterns of overachieving once again take control. Or we succumb to a subtle sort of pride that leads us to believe we can save ourselves as a result of our works. Or like the Pharisees, we fall into a practice of spiritual rites and legalism, which turn our works of love into routines of religion. Soon we become trapped in a compulsive behavior of performing works that were once the result of grace but have been changed by the desires of the flesh.

Are you caught in a cycle of trying harder and harder to please God, yet finding less and less comfort in the same? Do you feel spiritually drained and overworked? Is your spiritual work behavior becoming compulsive? Perhaps you need to step back from your works for God and begin again to marvel at the wonder of his grace. Don't work so hard. You've already received grace through your faith in him.

WHAT'S YOUR MOTIVE?

Jeff and Peggy recently left their church. You couldn't ask for a more dedicated family. He served faithfully in church leadership positions, directed the two semi-annual Saturday work days, taught Sunday School, and organized the men's retreat. Peggy led the new members' program, decorated for the Christmas service, was president of the choir, and often volunteered in the church office. Both of their children were leadership kids in the youth group, the oldest was most recently serving as president of the college/career group.

Why did they leave? According to some of their close friends, they left because they felt no one appreciated all of their hard work. They had been trying to gain a confirmation of God's acceptance through the affirmation of people in the church. With further investigation, it was discovered they had left their four previous churches for the same reason.

There are many families like this all over the country: people who serve the church, not *because* they are saved and want to joyfully give something to others, but because they are seeking appreciation and approval from church leaders and God. These people don't understand grace.

Please don't misunderstand me. The church would not be around today without faithful, giving servants like this family. But the motive of their service is the key. Perhaps the following advice given by a local pastor provides a good rule of thumb to follow with regard to service in the kingdom: "If you do it, don't resent it. If you resent it, don't do it!"

It is important to remember that although we are not saved by works, we should not see works for the sake of the gospel as bad. Quite the contrary is true. Ephesians 2:10 says, "For we are his workmanship, created in Christ Jesus for good works, which God prepared beforehand, that we should walk in them." So our good works are done through our relationship with Jesus Christ.

The story of the prodigal son in Luke 15 provides so many examples of God's love. The central theme is that of the father who welcomes back and celebrates a son who had moved away and squandered a fortune. But let's look at the brother of the lost son. He says to his father, "Look! For so many years I have been serving you, and I have never neglected a command of yours; and yet you have never given me a kid, that I might be merry with my friends; but when this son of yours came, who has devoured your wealth with harlots, you killed the fattened calf for him" (Lk 15:29-30). Have you ever caught yourself saying similar words? "It's just not fair, God. I work my fingers to the bone serving you. I teach Sunday school every week, lead a Bible study, serve as a deacon, and minister to shut-ins during the week. She's lucky if she shows up for church once in a while. Yet look at her. Everything seems to go her way, and I have more problems than anyone I know. It's just not fair."

And it probably isn't fair. Some people seem to have been dealt more than their share of hurts, failures, and emotional ailments. But God does not pass out problems based on the quantity or quality of our works. We are saved by grace through faith in him, and all other blessings come free of charge too. Our relationship with God is the greatest treasure of our lives. Our good works flow out of this love for

God. Colossians 3:23-24 says: "Whatever you do, do your work heartily, as for the Lord rather than for men; knowing that from the Lord you will receive the reward of the inheritance. It is the Lord Christ whom you serve."

GRACE-FUL EXERCISES

Changing our attitudes and behaviors with regard to works may be easy for some. Yet the longer we have been in a pattern of working toward heaven, the harder it may be for us to escape. Here are a few exercises that might help you evaluate and change your thinking regarding the free gift of grace we've received from God.

Step One: Evaluate your working habits. Think for a moment about the work you do each day. If you don't work outside the home, evaluate your role as housewife, consultant, or freelancer. Do you spend far too much time working in your daily activity? Is part of your motivation for working so hard that of avoiding pain and loneliness in your life or that of seeking approval from others? Or like Martha, do you feel as though you're doing more work than everyone else? Do you resent people who find other things more important than work? Are you *competitive*? Do you compare the work you do to the work of others? Do you take pride in the fact that you do a better job than those around you?

If you have any of these work habits, write two or three new goals. One might be to adjust your work schedule, another to be less competitive with others.

Step Two: Evaluate your works for God. In much the same way that you evaluated your work habits, consider the way these habits may affect the work you are doing for the kingdom of God. Perhaps you feel that your works really do get you a "better room in heaven." Maybe you feel you are doing most of the work in your church.

Only you can look at your specific situation and background. Use the following questions to help you evaluate your works for God. The more questions you answer yes to, the more you may need to realize God's grace as a free gift to you.

1. Do you find yourself doing things for the kingdom in an effort to guarantee your salvation, rather than doing them because of your salvation?

2. Do you find it difficult to say no when you are asked to volunteer for something, just because you think you may be letting God down?

3. Have you ever boasted to anyone about all the things you are doing in God's service?

4. As a child, did you feel that nothing you did was good enough for your parents? Now do you try to gain acceptance from God by overextending your service to him?

5. Is it difficult for you to believe that God has saved you through grace by your faith in him alone?

6. Do you feel guilty when you miss church, skip devotions, or otherwise break a pattern in your spiritual life?

7. Do you feel as though God cares for you less because you just don't meet his standards of performance?

8. Do you feel that the bad breaks have happened in your life because you just weren't spiritual enough?

Step Three: Seek God's guidance. Perhaps the Scriptures and examples in this chapter helped you receive a better understanding of God's grace. But no one can teach the real meaning or significance of this miraculous gift better than God can. In your search for grace, these healing habits are helpful:

1. Humble yourself before God with your honest need to know and understand him better. Surrender to him more profoundly, asking for his grace to change the areas where you need his help.
2. Thank God for the fact that his grace does in fact provide the glue that has made you whole and for the fact that you need him so completely.
3. Ask God to be glorified in your weakness.
4. Praise God for the fact that his grace works contrary to the ways of the world. Praise him because the more needy you become, the more abundant his grace is.

Step Four: Write a letter regarding God's free gift of grace. How difficult it is for many of us to accept God's grace as a gift. We've had to work for everything in our lives. The only way we can break bad habits is to start good habits to replace them. Try this final exercise as often as you can, and particularly whenever you feel like you are out of God's grace because you haven't worked hard enough.

Write a short letter or prayer to God on the wonder of his grace. You don't have to be an expert writer; this is for your own personal viewing and communication with God. In fact, since grace is such a simple gift, you should keep your letter as simple as possible. To get ideas use some of the key phrases illustrating grace on page 48.

If you don't feel like you have the creative juices to write anything at all, here's a simple sample for you to read.

Thank you, Lord, for saving me through your grace. It seems that I am not very good at accepting free gifts. I always feel that I have to do something to earn it. What a wonderful thing this grace is to me. You love me so much that all I have to do is believe in you and salvation is guaranteed.

You have declared me as righteous and holy, as well as forgiven me for all the times I've blown it. Your grace can replace these feelings of failure with feelings of purity and hope. Even when I did things I'm really ashamed of, your grace abounded even more to make up for it.

Help me, Lord, to do good works for you because of this wonderful gift, not in an effort to receive it. Allow me right now to stop everything I'm doing, close my eyes, and bask in the wonder of your love for me just as I am. Allow me to focus on that acceptance and grace for the next few minutes.

While Jesus hung on the cross, two thieves flanked him, also nailed to crosses. One scoffed at our Lord; the other repented of his sins. And to the latter Jesus replied, "Today you will be with me in Paradise." No works. No life patterned after strict laws. Just a convicted felon who asked for inclusion in the kingdom. It's free, absolutely free.

THREE

But
I'm Not
the One Who
Blew It!

✳ ✳ ✳

Stopping the Blame and Healing the Pain

For if you forgive men for their transgressions,
your heavenly Father will also forgive you.
But if you do not forgive men,
then your Father will not forgive your transgressions.

Mt 6:14-15 NAS

Habits that Hurt

Unforgiveness
Blaming others for our pain
Lacking trust

Symptoms

Bitterness
Resentment
Anger

Habits that Heal

Focusing on the forgiveness of God
Recognizing the positive in others
Taking responsibility for our actions

* * *

T HE NEWS WAS ALMOST TOO SHOCKING to reveal that terrifying August day in 1969. Investigators from the police department knew that it was only a matter of time before the press would be standing outside the gate of the exclusive home, equipped with their cameras, note pads, and microphones. Could the public even understand how something this shocking could happen? Soon they would know. Five people were dead. One, actress Sharon Tate, was eight months pregnant.

The Manson murders may go down in history as one of

the most shocking and gruesome events ever. Leno and Rosemary LaBianca were the victims in a killing spree the following night. The public began to panic, realizing that the events of the first night were not isolated murders. Months would pass before the complete truth would be known and the persons responsible placed behind bars. Families and friends of the people killed were devastated. Valuable lives that ended suddenly. Without reason. Tragically.

Suzan LaBerge was twenty-one years old at the time of the murders. Rosemary LaBianca was her mother, Leno her step-father. She had spent the day with them and had no idea that it would be her last. She and her fifteen-year-old brother discovered their bodies. Not only was she terrified that she could be the next victim, but the police were treating her as a possible suspect.

Can you imagine the trauma this young woman experienced? An article in *Christianity Today* says, "Within just a few weeks of the murders, LaBerge lost twenty-five pounds and dropped out of society. 'I didn't read the paper; I didn't watch TV. Later I began taking drugs and I ran around with the wrong crowd. I didn't talk to anyone about what had happened to my parents. I was so sick after the murders—paranoid, withdrawn, angry at God—I almost died.'"[1]

Now Suzan is a different person. And she explains that the one element that helped most in her recovery was her act of forgiving the murderers.

Shortly after giving her heart to the Lord, Suzan had seen a movie at church about prisoners who had made the same commitment. One of those new Christians was Charles "Tex" Watson, a member of the Manson family. And based on the Scriptures she had read, Suzan said that "since Jesus had forgiven me, and he had forgiven Charles Watson, I had to forgive Charles too."

Suzan began corresponding with Charles Watson though she did not reveal in the letters who she was. She also put her name on a waiting list to visit him. The day came when she was able to see him. After a short conversation, Suzan told Tex Watson her true identity. But she went a step further. She told the convicted man that she forgave him. "By then, we both had tears in our eyes. We held hands to pray together at the end of the visit, and I thought, 'These are no longer the hands that murdered my parents.'"

I would call Suzan's ability to forgive one that is far above the normal. Her life is not easy, and she has suffered various trials in the more than twenty years that have passed since her family's murder. To forgive Charles Watson is one thing; but she has gone on to build an ongoing relationship with him, still behind prison walls, and with his wife and his children outside. A remarkable example of forgiveness. Think about it for a moment. Who are the people in your life who need your forgiveness?

ANOTHER TYPE OF PAIN

For several years I have kept a note that brings a smile to my face. It is a plea for forgiveness from another segment of society, a nine-year-old boy. While the note was prompted by his parents, I still find the words sincere.

At the time I received this note, I was serving as the administrator for a church. Someone had vandalized a few of the signs around the church property. This is the letter I received, although it loses something being typeset rather than presented in its original handwritten form.

Dear Mr. Dreizler,

I'm sorry I broke the signs. I broke the signs because I was not thinking of others. I know you feel mad. I will donate my savings to the church. I feel disappointed in myself because it was wrong. I will respect others more. I will not damage other people's property again. I plan to tell others when I see them doings that are wrong. I feel sad for wrecking God's house of worship. I pray that God will forgive me. I pray that you and your church membership will forgive me also. I pray that Jesus forgive me also.

Your Friend

Perhaps this note means so much to me because it reminds me of an incident from my younger years. I was very active in the church youth group. Having attended almost every camp, weekly meeting, and social activity, I knew and was good friends with almost everyone in the group. One day we were going to a local Southern California amusement park and were encouraged to invite our nonchurchgoing friends as a type of outreach. I had invited some of my friends from the beach.

Shortly after arriving, one of the boys I was with stole something from one of the stores. Soon another took something. It became a game of who could take the most stuff. I held out for a while, but then the peer pressure caused me to give in too. We made it through most of the day. But a clever undercover guard saw one of the boys put something in his pocket. He waited until we were all together in a group and escorted us to the security area. It was the most humiliating day of my early youth.

But the real pain came later. Embarrassed by the situation, I quit going to the youth group. Somehow I thought that one of the many friends I had at the church—or at least one of the leaders—would call me and invite me back. No one ever did. In fact, when I saw one girl with whom I had become good friends at a local market, her mother told her not to talk to me because I was a bad kid. Now I know that I wasn't a bad kid, but for many years her comment made me feel that I was.

Unfortunately, the abandonment I felt was directed at the organized church for many years. I didn't attend church in high school or while at the University of Southern California. It was not until after college that I went to another church and rededicated my life to Jesus Christ. Shortly thereafter the pain of years of bitterness left me as I forgave the church and those who had never invited me back.

THE FEELING OF FORGIVENESS

Suzan LaBerge, just after forgiving Tex Watson, said, "I felt so light, so free, and so unburdened." That's much the way I felt when I decided to forgive the church. Years of anger and hurt seemed to flee from me.

Forgiveness for most deep hurts is a process and is rarely something that takes place overnight. For me, the forgiveness of the church took a decade. For one friend of mine, almost thirty years have passed since her father sexually abused her. And now that she's facing the issues, the forgiveness process is taking several years.

But the act of forgiveness is separate from the feeling of forgiveness. Sometimes the two events occur simultaneously, as it did for me. For my friend who was abused as a child, a recent letter from her dad asking for forgiveness has been the first step toward her feeling forgiveness.

When we mail a letter or otherwise confront someone who has wronged us, we must be prepared for the possibility that the abuser will not take ownership for his or her actions. The toughest forgiveness is that which doesn't rely on the response of the other. So don't be discouraged if your forgiveness of someone is not accompanied by feelings of joy and relief. It may take a long time for the bitterness to dissipate.

Quite often the feelings of forgiveness are truly experienced when the broken relationship has been reconciled. How glorious it is to be reunited with someone from whom we have been separated—whether the separation is for days, months, or years. Reconciliation is perhaps the best "happy ending" for people who are separated.

But even reconciliation is not a requirement for forgiveness. A person who is separated from another because of severe physical or emotional harm should feel no guilt in not being able to reconcile with a person directly. The further contact could cause more harm in their lives. It is possible, though not easy, to forgive an abuser and never have contact with him again. Nowhere in this chapter will I say that forgiveness is easy. But it's so healthy.

FORGIVE AND FORGET?

When a child touches a hot stove for the first time and burns her finger, she doesn't forget that the stove is a dangerous place to be. In much the same way, our ability to remember past hurts can keep us from further pain from the same or similar sources.

As we go through life, it is guaranteed that people are

going to hurt us. No one escapes this difficult byproduct of living with fellow human beings. Thankfully, we don't remember all of the hurts of our past. Some have been forgotten because they took place a long time ago. Others are forgotten because our love for the one who hurt us and our ability to forgive them is greater than the magnitude of the hurt done to us. But sometimes we can't forget the cause of the hurt even though we may have forgiven the one who hurt us. Our memory retains experiences that help us to avoid the same hurts in the future. Fortunately we can forgive those who have hurt us and be free from grudges without forgetting these lessons we've learned.

During a recent tour of the Salk Institute in San Diego, California, an institute that researches cures for terminal illnesses, a doctor told our group about the hippocampus, the part of the brain that allows us to store memories. It is the area of the brain currently being researched by those who are studying the causes of Alzheimer's Disease. When the hippocampus is injured or begins to deteriorate, the rest of the brain still allows us to see and function fine, but we are unable to create new memories. Wouldn't it be nice if we had such control over our hippocampus that we were able to regulate our memories, remembering the lessons we needed to keep but destroying the memories of past hurts and our own past sins once both have been forgiven?

If we are not able to forgive offenses against us, we begin to carry the bitterness around. Like a large boulder that partially blocks the flow of a river, the lack of forgiveness begins to block the flow of our relationships. We become guarded, afraid of being hurt by someone else. With each day that passes, with each new moment of resentment, another boulder is heaped on until a dam has reached from shore to shore, allowing only the smallest trickle of joy to continue flowing.

As Christians it seems that we would somehow be spared from the pain of interpersonal failures, betrayals, and disappointments. But this is just not the case. In fact, in many ways it becomes more painful when the ones hurting us are fellow believers: the pastor at our church, the person we taught Sunday school with for years, the neighbor who was in our home fellowship, the best friend we met when we served on the elder board together, the guy we sat next to in seminary.

As resentment builds within us when we refuse to forgive someone, sometimes we unwillingly vent the frustration by releasing the anger at another person. This might be a family member, a friend, or a complete stranger. We might even blame God for the hurt.

Anthony was filled with anger in finding out that his best friend had betrayed him. After a week his anger did not dissipate; in fact, it grew even more intense. While looking for a parking place in a full lot, he noticed a car backing out. After waiting for the car to drive away another driver came from the other direction and took the parking place.

Normally the mild-mannered Anthony might shake his head in frustration and move on to search for another space. But that day he jumped out of his car and shouted at the other driver face-to-face. When he got back into his car, Anthony was shaking. His reaction that day was so unlike his usual behavior, he realized that he had to do something to free himself from the hurt of the recent broken relationship. Forgiveness was the only answer. How much greater is the need to forgive for those who have carried pain and bitterness for months, for years. Yet forgiving is not all that easy.

BARRIERS TO FORGIVENESS

Most of the obstacles to spiritual growth presented in this book are tough issues. It would be so easy if we could just wave a magic wand and somehow have the feelings of resentment, shame, and disappointment removed from our lives. But part of the complexity of any emotion we feel is that God has created each one of us different from the other.

Some people are able to quickly forgive those who hurt them. This ability may be something that comes naturally to them, or it may stem from a mature walk with the Lord. For those who find it hard to forgive, the root of the problem may be one of the following.

Unrealistic expectations. Perhaps those of us who have the hardest struggle with forgiving others are those who forget about the fallen nature of mankind. We sometimes expect ourselves and others to be good all the time. When we fail or someone fails us, that expectation is shattered, and we shift into feelings that we or the person who failed us is all bad. Once we come to terms with the truth that no one is perfect, we can begin on the road that leads to health and maturity.

Part of forgiveness is realizing that the people in our lives will let us down. Even our loved ones will forget birthdays, say hurtful things, move away from us emotionally, and otherwise disappoint us. But when the bad part of someone emerges, we must remember that the good parts of the person are still there too.

Remember in the last chapter when I said how important grace is to all of the themes in this book? Well, here is an example of its importance. For just as Christ values you and me despite the way we turn from him, so should we show grace to others when they come up short of our expectations.

A history of hurts. For some, the inability to forgive is based on a life full of betrayals and hurts. We use an unforgiving heart as a defense mechanism to move away from people.

Sometimes they are people who care for and love us. Yet we move away because we think the pain of isolation is less hurtful than the pain of another betrayal or abandonment.

Experts say that a large part of our adult personality is formed during the early years of childhood. The events we experience and the environment to which we are exposed as children play a significant role in our lives as adults. Maybe you had a near-perfect childhood. On the other hand, if you were abused or neglected during your younger years, perhaps you have carried a lack of trust into your adult years. You may have been raised to be a perfectionist, and now you are dealing with a spouse who is less than perfect. Or maybe you always got your way as a child, and now that your boss won't let you do what you want, you seethe with anger and resentment toward him.

The "history of hurts" may have continued into your adult years. Perhaps your first marriage was a failure. Then your pastor ran off with the church secretary. Your boss took an idea of yours and made thousands of dollars without ever rewarding you. At your twenty-year reunion you discovered that your long-lost friend is now married to your ex-spouse—and they'd had a relationship for years before you were even divorced.

Do these things happen in the world? You bet. Do they happen in the Christian community? Unfortunately they do. No matter how hard we try to shield ourselves from the pain and betrayal of human relationships, they still happen. We cannot prevent other people from hurting us. But we can choose to move on.

Try to release these hurts. If they are too deep for you to face, ask a professional or a trustworthy friend for help. Your unforgiving heart is not affecting the people who hurt you; it is robbing you of a joyful and whole life.

Blaming others. When some injustice comes into our lives, we often place one hundred percent of the blame on the other person. But every divorce, every friendship, every working relationship, involves the interaction of two people. In almost every case where a rift has taken place, there is fault on both sides. We don't want to admit this when we've been hurt badly, but it's true.

Is the blame always fifty-fifty? Of course not. Unfortunately, there are some people in this world who are just plain difficult. Certain qualities such as greed, self-centeredness, anger, and the like make them almost impossible to deal with. But in any relationship we must also look at ourselves.

Think about a person you've never forgiven. For a moment, stop the finger-pointing and try to remember a time when you failed him or her. All of us have hurt those closest to us in some way or another. We've said something that hurt their feelings; we've persisted with some habit that annoys them; we've turned our back on them when they needed us the most. Take responsibility for what you've done to hurt the relationship.

Perhaps you have a long list of failed relationships and have always blamed the other parties for the failures. Time after time you have driven people away; yet your response remains, "Boy, she really had problems." Perhaps you'll see the person who really has the problems next time you look in the mirror.

Consider the following as indicators that you may be denying some problems within your own personality and ability to relate with others:

- You've been divorced more than once.
- The company or department you run has a lot of turnover.

- Your social engagements with friends are few and far between.
- Many people seem to resent you or be angry with you.
- You make excuses when people question your decisions or behavior.
- You're constantly trying to figure out what's wrong with everyone else.

If you suspect that you need help, you've made the first step toward a better life for yourself and those around you. Seek help. And then, while you learn to forgive others, perhaps you can ask others whom you've hurt to forgive you. Reconciliation is a wonderful and fulfilling part of life.

Unrealistic expectations, past hurts, and blaming others for your problems are just a few of the roots of an unforgiving heart. Perhaps you can relate to one of these causes. Or perhaps you have an unforgiving heart only because no one ever taught you how to forgive. I hope some of the Scriptures and suggestions in this chapter will help you move toward the goal of forgiving others who have hurt you. It's the best thing you can do for yourself.

GOD'S WORD ON FORGIVENESS

My favorite example of forgiveness is found in the life of Joseph in the Old Testament. Genesis 37-50 tell the story of his life. Joseph was betrayed by his own brothers, sold into slavery, and taken to Egypt. There his master's wife told others that Joseph had slept with her, and he was sent to jail.

I'm sure these betrayals hurt Joseph. Those closest to him prevented him from living a life he should have lived, close to his father, friends, and loved ones. But God used the evil of Joseph's brothers for the good of mankind. He made Joseph a leader in Egypt and allowed him to help thousands of people who would have otherwise died.

Joseph saw God's hand in his circumstances and forgave his brothers from his heart. He welcomed them to Egypt and provided a good life for them while their own land suffered famine. Forgiving isn't easy. If you are bitter right now, you may not realize that God has great things planned for you too.

Throughout the Bible there are many personal examples, parables, and verses that stress the important role forgiveness must play if we are to grow in our love for Jesus Christ and for one another. The Lord's Prayer includes the lines, "And forgive us our debts, as we forgive our debtors" (Mt 6:12). Jesus links our need to forgive others with the forgiveness that the Father provides to each one of us, just as he does in Matthew 6:14-15. Perhaps he did this to help us in the forgivness process. At first we may find it nearly impossible to forgive someone who has deeply hurt us. And in fact, it may be impossible for us to forgive someone without God's help. But when we reflect upon the thousands of things for which God has forgiven us over the years, maybe we can learn from him and forgive others for the harm they have done to us.

The forgiveness process yields an interesting cycle. On the one hand, we must learn from God's forgiveness so that we too might have the spiritual strength to forgive those who have hurt us. On the other hand, Scripture tells us that we cannot be forgiven until we have forgiven others. Think about a time when you were unable to forgive someone. You may have someone in mind as you read this. When you harbor those feelings of bitterness, can you honestly say that you feel the overwhelming forgiveness of God? Of course not. We must learn from the forgiveness of God and in turn forgive others. Only then are we free to know the true spirit of human and divine forgiveness.

Jesus further illustrates our need to forgive in the story of the unforgiving steward who refused to forgive a small debt owed to him after he had been forgiven for a large debt owed to another (Mt 18:23-35). It is interesting that Jesus told this story in response to a question from Peter, "Lord, how often shall my brother sin against me and I forgive him? Up to seven times?" Jesus responded, "I do not say to you, up to seven times, but up to seventy times seven."

By now it should be evident that God demands that we freely forgive one another if we are to be right with him. The great Oswald Chambers said, "The love of God is based on justice and holiness, and I must forgive on the same basis."

FACING FORGIVENESS IN OUR LIVES

How can we forgive the people in our lives who have harmed us? Because of the factors we talked about in this chapter, each person will find different things useful in the forgiving process. Here are a few exercises and suggestions that might help you forgive others in your life.

Step One: Focus on the forgiveness of God. Before you try to forgive others, focus on the things discussed in the Scripture section above. Realize the miraculous forgiveness that has been given to you by God. There is no end to the love he has in forgiving you time and time again. Unlike most of us, he not only forgives our wrongdoing, he forgets it!

There has never been a greater display of forgiveness than the crucifixion of Christ on the cross. If you are bitter and angry at someone for the way they hurt you and are afraid of the pain it may take to forgive them, consider the pain Jesus went through so that we might all be forgiven of our sins forever. Forgiveness is not easy for us, and the cross certainly wasn't easy for Jesus. Yet through his life and lessons we have the ability to forgive the worst of sins committed against us. In fact, it's required for our continued forgiveness in return.

Fill in the blanks below:

If God can forgive me for the times I _____ _____ and _____ and _____, and _____ _____, surely I can forgive others for the things they have done to me.

Step Two: Identify those whom you need to forgive. Using the chart below, think carefully about all of the people in your life whom you need to forgive. (For privacy you may want to record your thoughts on a separate sheet of paper.) You may be surprised at how many come to mind. Keep in mind that forgiving a person does not necessarily mean that you will restore your relationship to what it once was. In some situations this is not possible or wise.

Forgiving Worksheet

I, _____, need to forgive the following people:

Name   **Offense against**

_____ for _____

_____ for _____

Name	Offense against
_____	for _____
_____	for _____
_____	for _____
_____	for _____

Step Three: Realize the good in each person. Now that you've listed all the ways that this person has hurt you, list all their positive qualities. Remember that everyone has a good part within them too.

Name	Good Qualities
_____	is _____
_____	is _____
_____	is _____
_____	is _____
_____	is _____
_____	is _____

Step Four: Realize your part in each situation. For each person you listed above, list the things that you did that might have contributed to the painful situation. Again, you may want to follow the format shown below but make your list on a separate sheet of paper.

For example, let's say that one of the persons you listed is a former friend whose selfishness destroyed your relationship. Focus in this section on the things you might have done to hurt her also. Your response may go something like this, "To Margaret. I often resented your children because I don't have any. And I wasn't there when you most needed me—guess I was selfish too!"

Special Note: If you were the victim of abuse, rape, molestation, or some other crime, you should not complete this section regarding your offenses against the person to be forgiven. Too many innocent victims of such crimes struggle for years with feelings of self-blame and guilt when they did absolutely nothing to deserve such treatment. I hope this book will help in some way as you seek freedom from any self-blame you still feel.

Name	Offense against
To _____	I _____
To _____	I _____
To _____	I _____
To _____	I _____
To _____	I _____
To _____	I _____

Do you notice any common patterns here? Are there things about you that others have told you, yet you keep denying? List those personal attributes that you plan to work on in the coming months (or years):

_____

_____

_____

_____

_____

Step Five: Let go of the hurt. Now that you've identified those who have hurt you, reviewed the good in each of them, and listed your own shortcomings in each situation, you have an outline to write a letter to each one.

Try to express your feelings. Tell the person how they hurt you. But in addition, list the things you did wrong and ask for their forgiveness too. Mention all the positive things that you see in this person and the fact that God too sees them as someone he loves.

If this sounds scary to you, realize that you do not have to mail the letter to this person. Sending such a letter to some people may even worsen the relationship. You can write your letter, seal it, and put it away to collect dust. Whether you decide to send the letter or not, this exercise is designed to provide a way for you to express your feelings. Even if the person is someone you haven't seen in thirty years or if the person is deceased, you can write this letter.

In some cases, you may want to restore the relationship and mail either this letter or one that is toned down a bit. If so, do not get your expectations up. The other person may not want to restore the relationship with you. You may never hear from them again. If they do call to reconcile, you will be pleasantly surprised. In any case, the important thing is to forgive them and move on to a fresh new start.

Writing a letter is only one means of expressing forgiveness. It may be possible to sit down with the person and talk about your relationship. Some have forgiven people who have abused them by volunteering to help other people heal from being abused themselves. Forgiveness might involve a series of such actions. Letting go of the hurt may not be easy in especially hurtful situations. If you feel you can't do it on your own, seek professional help from a therapist, group, or even a caring in-patient program.

Forgiving: perhaps something against our human nature, but an act filled with the freedom and love upon which our Christian faith is based. Start the process of forgiving others in your life today.

FOUR

The Butterfly Who Thought He Was Still a Caterpillar

* * *

Accepting the New Creation

Therefore if any man is in Christ, he is a new creature; the old things passed away; behold, new things have come.   **2 Cor 5:17 NAS**

Habits that Hurt

Shame
Self-abuse
Focusing on external appearance

Symptoms

Negative talk about oneself
Feelings of rejection
Chronic depression

Habits that Heal

Treating our bodies as temples of God
Forgiving ourselves
Accepting ourselves as new creations
Celebrating our uniqueness

✳ ✳ ✳

L ISA WAS A VERY LOVELY AND TALENTED WOMAN, but she didn't feel lovely at all. She had a secret she had ever told anyone, not even her husband of eighteen years.

The daughter of a prominent pastor in the community, at the age of sixteen, led a very pure life. But one night she and her boyfriend went too far. Lisa became pregnant. Ashamed and scared of what the community would think, she began to look for a way out. Even though abortion was not yet legal in her state and Lisa felt this was a morally wrong decision, she found a person who would terminate the pregnancy for her.

Scared and filled with guilt, Lisa showed up for her appointment. The procedure itself didn't take long. While she lay down in the recovery area, Lisa began to cry. Not only did she feel like her insides had been ripped out, she felt as though part of her soul was gone. On the way home she had to pull over to the side of the road several times, for she was crying too hard to drive. Because of complications, Lisa was in physical pain for several weeks following the abortion. But the emotional scars stayed with her for years beyond.

Twenty-three years later, Lisa still saw herself as a terrible person. Now she was like a butterfly who emerged from a cocoon long ago when she accepted Christ, yet she never really lifted her wings to fly because she still saw herself as she used to be. For years she had allowed her self-esteem to be affected by the sins of her life—before and after her life with Jesus Christ. Every time something negative happened, she saw it as continued punishment for something she did many years ago. She didn't realize that God doesn't work this way.

Lisa had a very big heart when it came to forgiving others, but she had never forgiven herself or accepted the forgiveness of Christ. Although it would take some time for her to rebuild her self-esteem and see what a truly fine woman she was, Lisa was ready to begin the process.

Sometimes we are so hard on ourselves because we fail. But we are not perfect. Our perfection can only be found in the forgiveness of Jesus Christ. Lisa needed to celebrate the new creation that was formed when she first accepted Jesus. He'd been waiting a long time to see the butterfly take wing.

THE DAMAGED SELF-WORTH

After working closely with prisoners, the homeless, and people in psychiatric hospitals, it is apparent to me that there is one common thread among most of those who are hurting. That thread is low self-esteem. And there are just as many people walking around churches, middle-class neighborhoods, and university campuses who suffer from low self-esteem.

Very few people go through life without struggling with their self-worth at one time or another. Even people who come from model homes and who have never suffered from neglect, abuse, or family dysfunction can face times when they question their worth as human beings. Sometimes low self-worth is generated by a long series of little disappointments rather than a few traumatic events.

Low self-esteem can totally debilitate one, even to the point of believing her life is not worth living. Other people function very well despite nagging feelings of falling short of their own expectations. And there are degrees of self-esteem problems everywhere between these scenarios.

As mentioned in the previous chapter, much of our personality and self-worth is formed during the early childhood years. Toby's life shows how early circumstances can carry over into adulthood. Toby was only six years old when his father abandoned him and his family. Just two years later, his mother became very ill and died. Toby, his brother, and his sisters were taken to different foster homes. During his childhood years, Toby would move on to different families many times. Each time he began to trust one of the families with whom he stayed, the people from the agency would come and send him to another home. As Toby grew older, he became more and more of a loner. It seemed safer for him. Everyone he had ever loved had either abandoned him, died, or moved away.

When he entered high school, Toby retreated further. Skinny and lanky, the other kids made fun of him. He was always chosen last when picking teams in physical education class.

By the time Toby entered college, he had filled out and was a nice-looking young man. And in the new environment with new people around him, Toby found that people began speaking to him. While his social life improved, Toby made sure that he never got too close to anyone. On the outside he seemed like a normal, healthy young man. Yet on the inside Toby was an empty six-year-old boy huddled in the corner of the room, crying and afraid. He did not feel loved or lovable.

As he grew further into adulthood, Toby's isolation seemed to worsen. He feared the feelings of abandonment would haunt him until the day he died. He pictured himself waking up one day as a feeble old man—still alone and still afraid to let anyone in.

Denise's story is much different. Raised in an upper-middle-class part of town, she had everything she could have wanted. Her parents had a very good marriage and both spent a great deal of time with her. Denise was very beautiful. During her high school years, she became quite popular and was crowned queen of the senior prom.

As she entered college and joined a sorority, however, Denise began to have problems. Suddenly there were many other beautiful women around. No longer was she the center of attention. Slowly Denise's self-worth began to deteriorate. She became obsessed with the need for the same attention she had received in high school. This need led her to a promiscuous lifestyle.

Then she began striving to obtain the perfect body. Denise hardly ate anything. And when she did, she purged or ingested diuretics to rapidly remove the food from her body. Before long Denise's weight had reached a dangerously low point. The once queen of the prom was now a very sick young woman who believed that beauty lay in a sleek body and her worth depended on her sexual escapades. Before long Denise hit rock bottom, then began a continuing struggle to regain her self-worth.

People with low self-esteem come from all income levels and backgrounds. A low self-image can take the richest of the rich to the streets or place the mightiest in power behind prison bars. Why are there so many people who hurt so badly? There are a number of contributing factors. I believe that our society's loss of moral values is a very significant one. Premarital sex has become an acceptable lifestyle, even to many in the Christian church. Those seeking abortion used to be the ones breaking the law: now those who try to stop babies from being killed are arrested. The New Age movement has provided new idols, so that people who think they are worshiping God are actually worshiping something totally unrelated to him. An astronomical divorce rate has shattered families. As we drift further from God and his truth, we lose the sense of our own value. Instead of seeking our worth in his love and forgiveness, we try to find worth in material things and relationships. We become self-centered rather than Christ-centered.

HOW DOES LOW SELF-WORTH AFFECT US?

Perhaps you were able to identify with Lisa, Toby, or Denise in one way or another. Even though your circumstances are not exactly the same as any of these three, do you:

- continue to beat up on yourself for the mistakes you made years ago?
- believe that the negative things that happen to you are God's punishment for sin?
- hate yourself for what you've done or for being who you are?

- still believe you personify the names people called you as a child?
- have a history of little disappointments?
- feel you are not worthy of love because of past abandonments or neglect?
- look in the mirror with feelings of disgust or shame?
- feel you've received more than your fair share of hard knocks?
- have feelings of anxiety when you realize that something you've done isn't perfect?
- allow the actions or comments of others to influence how you feel about yourself?
- lack confidence in your ability to work, interact, or relate with others well?
- blame yourself because of some past failed relationships?
- think of yourself as less intelligent or less attractive than the majority of other people?

If you answered yes to any of these questions, you may have low self-esteem. Perhaps you need to learn to forgive, accept, and love yourself—to see yourself as the unique person God created. Your family, friends, and job are probably important aspects of your life. You should be aware that if you suffer from low self-esteem, you are cheating them all out of a better relationship by offering them only a part of the person you really are.

Far beyond the limitations to personal relationships, low self-esteem can be one of the greatest barriers to spiritual growth and a close relationship with God. With all the shame Lisa felt, she was afraid to go before God. Her inability to accept God's forgiveness kept her from a close relationship with him. Toby had trouble believing that God really loved him. The abandonment of his own father, combined with the name-calling of his peers early in life, had convinced him that he was unworthy of anyone's love—even God's.

Finally, a poor self-image can lead people down many dangerous roads—alcoholism, severe depression, drug addiction, failed relationships, violence, suicidal thoughts. Even though some of these things have physiological components, quite often low self-esteem draws people into these problems.

If you have a poor self-image, whether it is caused by abuse someone else inflicted upon you, your appearance, your inability to forgive some past mistakes, or any other factors, I hope that this chapter will help you begin your journey to inner peace and a greater love of yourself. Some people might need to ask a qualified therapist to help them on this journey. Life is too short to spend it as someone you don't like.

BUT SHOULD I LOVE MYSELF?

Before we go too far, let me clarify what I mean by a love of self. Better stated, let me say what self-love is not. Self-love is not a "me first" or selfish attitude of life. Nor is self-love synonymous with self-centeredness. Usually people who are egotistical and self-centered must build themselves up because of certain insecurities in their lives, not because they are overly self-confident. A self-love that pushes away and offends others is not a healthy self-love.

Self-love is present when a person's first priority is to see himself through the eyes of the Father, despite the sins and shortcomings of his past. It is the ability of a person to see his value, not in the success of his business or the acceptance of his peers, but in the forgiving and open arms of love extended by Jesus Christ. We believe we are worthy because we accept the value of ourselves as assigned by God, who made us in his image and wants an intimate relationship with us for all eternity. A person with true self-love is one who has a high regard for herself or himself yet is fully aware of weakness and limitations.

Our relationship with Christ helps us see ourselves as he sees us: created in his image and, though fallen with the rest of man, forgiven and loved as special creations. For some committed Christians this process may take many years. Unfortunately, some who truly love Christ never accept themselves because they have never been willing to confront the barriers to that acceptance. Do I care enough about myself that I will seek help to change the things I don't like?

If your second priority is the service of others, *and* that service is being done with humility, your self-esteem will be further enhanced through your servanthood. Helping others provides a way for you to pass on the acceptance you receive from God to others who might need to see a glimpse of his love. It also helps move you away from self-centeredness. Finally, you must be kind to yourself as one who needs rest and time for pleasure.

This "me third" approach to life should not create one who is a "doormat," who allows others to take advantage of him or her. Someone with good self-esteem is able to detect people who see him or her as a doormat and confront them. Being other-centered does not mean we deny relational problems or cover them up. This is a sign of codependency, a product of low self-esteem.

GOALS TO GO FOR

Think of yourself for a moment as someone who is filled with the *joy* of being unconditionally loved by Christ, the *peace* of walking with the Holy Spirit, and the *freedom* to love others unconditionally because God loves you unconditionally. Can you see yourself going through each day for the rest of your life experiencing these things? If not, think of all the baggage you carry: abuse, an undesirable physical characteristic, abandonment, sin, feelings of worthlessness. God wants so much for you to shed all that baggage and realize the joy, peace, and freedom you have in Christ. I hope as you read these pages that you can identify the baggage that keeps you from enjoying life.

To put it as simply as possible, the goal of this chapter is to encourage you to move closer to:

- being able to forgive yourself for a lifestyle you are no longer a part of.
- loving yourself for exactly who you are, complete with your imperfections.
- changing the things that are blocking you from having a positive self-image.
- judging your success by Jesus' standards rather than the world's standards.
- celebrating your uniqueness.
- seeing yourself as a new creature, letting the old pass away.
- realizing that you will never be alone, abused, or abandoned by God.

Gaining a better self-image is a process that usually cannot happen overnight. But today is as good a day as any to evaluate how you view yourself. We can either wallow in the pain, circumstances, and misfortunes of the past and allow them to depress, defeat, and belittle our self-worth, or we can choose to begin a new life and claim victory over all of the things in our past that have kept us from really appreciating who we are.

Again I must emphasize how important the acceptance of God's grace is to our becoming unstuck in any area. Unless we are able to view ourselves in the eyes of Christ, who sees us as a treasure that's beyond any value, we will continue to see ourselves as empty and invaluable. You must find your joy in his love. No matter what you've done or what names you have been called, Christ's love is infinitely more powerful and affirming than all the things that drag you down.

EXAMINING OUR BAGGAGE

Let's examine some of the factors that influence people's self-worth in a negative way. Perhaps you find some of these in the baggage that weighs you down.

Physical abuse. How would you stereotype one who batters another human being? You might picture a poor, uneducated male, wearing a tank-top undershirt and sporting whiskers. But, physically abusive people are found wearing expensive suits in law offices, leading PTA meetings, sitting quietly in church pews, and frequenting elite social clubs. These people can walk through life without being known as abusers, simply because their victims do not want to expose them.

If you talk with people who have been abused, a great many will actually believe that they deserved it. This is where the pattern of low self-esteem begins for the physically abused person. He might subconsciously say, "I can see why she hit me. I misbehaved, and I'm not a very good son." Then this thinking turns to, "I should be hit because I'm worthless." As this thought continues with further abuse, the abused person can actually believe that he or she is worthless in the eyes of others, themselves, and even God. This might be why many who have been abused as children grow up to marry an abusive spouse.

Neglect or abandonment. In some cases, children feel neglected, abandoned, or rejected because parents have left the home and had little or no further contact with the son or daughter. The child often struggles with the thought that the missing parent might have left because of her. But children can suffer from neglect though both parents live at home. Some parents place their children as a low priority with regard to their time schedule. Extensive travel either for business or pleasure may take them away from home for extended periods of time. Being overcommitted to work or other obligations can result in the same thing.

Time away from children may not in itself cause feelings of neglect. Many jobs require a great deal of time away from the home. But if the parents continue to remain distant and too busy to spend quality time with the children even when they are home, the children may interpret this lack of attention as a lack of love. Further, they may internalize the situation by seeing themselves as unlovable.

Often these children will do almost anything to get their parents' attention. Some excel by becoming overachievers, hoping Mom and Dad will reward them with their time and attention. Others, unfortunately, seek attention by getting into trouble. They end up at the principal's office or at the police station, but at least they get to spend time with their parents when they come to pick them up. Still others seek attention from someone else, since they cannot get any at home. Too often the confused adolescent thinks he or she can find the lost love and intimacy through sexual encounters. The activity leads to even lower self-esteem.

Verbal abuse. I'm amazed at some of the things I hear parents say to their children in public.

- "You're worthless."
- "I wish you were never born."
- "You'll never amount to anything."
- "You're just like your father, fat and lazy."
- "I'm going to trade you in for a kid who behaves."
- "If it weren't for you, I wouldn't have to work all these hours."
- "Right now keeping my job is more important than your silly baseball game."
- "I wish you were like the Collins children. They are so smart and talented."

Believe it or not, parents actually say these things to their kids during the delicate years when the foundation of their self-worth is being formed. Perhaps you heard them from your parents, grandparents, or other influential adults in your life. These words sting. They affect our self-esteem. And they are words that can stay with us for years.

Substance abuse. When parents are involved in addictions, the dysfunction affects the entire family. We will talk more about dependencies in the next chapter; here I want to point out that the substance abuse of parents can greatly affect the self-worth of the child. The child often sees himself as the one from whom Dad is escaping when he drinks or uses drugs. Children who are raised by alcoholics commonly suffer from some of the abandonment issues we discussed earlier. And the chemicals taken in by the abuser can make other types of abuse more likely.

Perfectionism or high standards. Parents who strive for perfection will most likely be disappointed if they expect the same from their children. A child who returns the hammer to the garage might be praised by some parents for being a good boy. But the perfectionist parent may scold him instead because he put the hammer in the wrong drawer. The child begins to believe that he can do nothing right. A little girl who is punished for bringing home her first "C" on her report card in a subject she finds difficult will feel that being average in something is wrong. If this happens enough, chances are she will feel less than worthy if she doesn't reach the ultimate in other things as she goes through life.

Sexual abuse. Grandpa is coming to take Molly to the zoo. Instead of being excited, the little girl is crying and telling her mother that she doesn't want to go. When her fear results in a tantrum, her mother tries to calm her, "You don't want to hurt Grandpa's feelings, do you?" Afraid that Grandpa might hurt her even more if she told her mom about the scary things he did to her, Molly turns and walks out the door with her grandfather. As they drive away she looks out the back window of the car, wondering why Mommy allows it to go on.

Studies show that at least one in five girls and one in ten boys will be sexually abused before they reach the age of eighteen. Even though almost all molestations take place through no fault of the victim, he or she is the one who pays most for the crime through psychological scars, added fears, and usually a severely damaged self-image. And since the molesting person is usually a relative or friend of the family, the abused one often has trouble trusting people in authority throughout life. A staggering number of people who are perpetrators of violent crime were molested as children.

Frequent teasing. I remember myself as a ninety-pound fresh-man at Redondo Union High School, the shortest male in the class. Several of the "jocks" would point fingers and call me names like "Pansy," "Wimp," and "Shorty." This is not one of my favorite memories from childhood, but it certainly is one that shaped my self-image for many years beyond that time.

"Sticks and stones will break my bones, but words will never hurt me." Chances are we all heard that phrase when we were little children. Unfortunately, it's simply not true. Words can hurt us much more than sticks and stones by destroying our self-confidence. And the emotional "bones" that are broken take much longer to heal than do most physical ailments we face. As adults we are more equipped to handle it when others call us names, yet insults and name-calling still hurt our very being.

Almost all of us were called names at one time or another. But the most frequent targets of teasing are those who are different in some way. Toby was called "Bean Pole" and "Toothpick" because of his lanky body. Some were teased because they were heavier than most kids. Others had complexion problems. Perhaps an exaggerated facial feature such as a big nose or "Dumbo" ears caused kids to point and laugh at you.

Physical characteristics. Recently I came across the Miss America contest on television. It didn't take me long to pick out Miss Hawaii as my favorite. I found that the judges felt the same way, for Miss Hawaii did indeed win. She is a very pretty and talented young woman.

This was a beauty contest, so it makes sense that a beautiful woman won. Unfortunately, many of life's "contests," such as those for popularity, are judged the same way. It seems like the attractive people get the most dates, the most attention, and the most opportunities.

The favoring of the best-looking people begins with the earliest stages of life. A study several years ago traced the reactions of adults who were brought into various situations with one cute little boy and one not-so-cute little boy. The children were tracked via hidden camera as they went into clothing stores with their mothers, attended preschool, or walked through the park. In almost every case, the cute little boy was given far more attention than the unattractive one. People wanted to pick him up, pat him on the head, or simply talk to him. Affirming comments regarding the little boy's appearance were made to the boy's mother, while the other mother stood by without any comments directed to her son. As one who loves children, I was moved by the story. And it makes me think twice when I see a little child who is not so cute.

It is very difficult not to allow our own physical features to affect how we think about ourselves. Keeping a proper perspective on the definition of beauty in God's eyes is very important to us as Christian people. But this worldly ideal of physical beauty is a very tough mold from which to escape— as we view others *and* ourselves.

The comparison trap. Imagine a tired-looking man standing on the front lawn of his modest home. He watches carefully as the people he grew up and went to college with go by. One drives a new luxury car. Another walks by wearing a custom-made suit. Still another drives by and asks if he'd like to go sailing on his new yacht. Filled with feelings of envy and failure, the man turns with his head down and enters his home.

The comparison game is a dangerous activity, and what is at risk is our own self-worth. It is frustrating to tie up our self-worth in the number of goods we have compiled or the size of our home, because in the comparison game, there will always be something nicer and bigger. As Christians we are to praise God for blessing us with possessions, but our contentment must be found in a close relationship with him.

This comparison game seems to be most prevalent in fast-paced areas like the major cities. I know so many who are playing it. They buy the most expensive and top-label dress for the upcoming social event, even if they can't afford it. After all, what would people think if they wore the same dress as at the last function? I once heard a member of one of America's wealthiest families say on television that she'd rather be crying in a Rolls Royce than laughing on a bicycle. In this comparison game, I'll take the bicycle any day.

Being alone. As a former singles pastor, I realize how many people really grieve over their marital status. Divorce recovery workshops have been created to help those who feel rejected or unworthy because a mate has decided to move on. Some of those who have never married feel that they're just not worth anything to anyone. And many who are married suffer because a spouse belittles them in one way or another.

Singleness is not incompleteness, and marriage is not the place to find your self-worth. The successful marriages I know are those where both spouses feel complete as individuals, both are centered in Jesus Christ, and each honors the other above himself or herself. The single people I know who are content with their lives are those who are also grounded in Christ and who have found wholeness apart from seeking it in another human being. Others can help lead us to a stronger self-image, but they cannot give it to us. We can find it only in the eyes of God.

Our past sins. In the previous chapter we talked about the bad habit of not forgiving others. Now we look at the bad habit of not forgiving ourselves. Again, the inability to understand and accept the grace of God presents a barrier to our spiritual growth.

Lisa, in our opening story, is holding back a part of herself from the persons she loves and from God. She cannot understand how her wretchedness can be forgiven. She refuses to put her sin behind her.

The perfectionist who wants to live a life without sin will always fail, because we all sin. Such people beat up their self-worth each time they refuse to forgive their own past, strive for absolute perfection, or don't believe that their sin is behind them.

PORTRAITS OF SELF-WORTH

Imagine yourself standing in a room of a unique art gallery—unique because the walls of this room are lined with paintings that depict your life from the moment you were born until now. Hopefully, most of the paintings will be happy and colorful, but perhaps there will be some paintings that show some of the baggage we just discussed.

All of the paintings in your gallery went into creating the person you are today. If most of them are ugly because of a tragic past, you unfortunately cannot change them. But you can change the way the paintings look from here on out. The paintings of your past are not as important as the way you've learned from them and are able to begin painting more cheerful portraits from here on out.

Changing the way we feel about ourselves is like any other habit—it takes time. If you think very little of yourself, it is because that self-defeating attitude has been with you for a very long time. Some events from your childhood have set you in that pattern, and certain consequences of adulthood may have contributed even further. But you *can* change.

GOD SAYS SO

As Christians, we have the benefit of finding comfort in the Word of God. Paul, who saw himself as the worst of all sinners, provides many encouraging words to the one with low self-esteem.

The Scripture at the beginning of this chapter encourages us: "Therefore if any man is in Christ, he is a new creature; the old things passed away; behold, new things have come" (2 Cor 5:17). Similarily, Jesus told Nicodemus that to see the kingdom of God, we must be born again, born of the Spirit.

Some people have miraculous conversions to Christ. The "new creature," "born again" of the Spirit, emerges as naturally as a butterfly comes forth from its cocoon. But others have found that the new life in Christ has grown only with patience and endurance.

If we truly believe the words of Paul in 2 Corinthians, then it seems we should be able to erase the problems of the past that affected our self-worth. Unfortunately, the human side of us remembers. We remember the abuse, name-calling, lack of beauty, and all of the other things that pull us down. Those elements of the old creature come back to haunt us at times.

We must try to focus more on what Scripture says about us. Then we can see ourselves as a new creation and learn to forget the old, just as God does.

ONE WOMAN'S NEW BEGINNING

It must have been quite a scene. Jesus, coming down from the Mount of Olives, crossed the small valley and entered the temple where people were gathering to hear him teach. While he was speaking, a commotion arose from the back of the crowd. A group of scribes and Pharisees pulled a woman toward him. They threw her down near the feet of Jesus, and she hid her face in humiliation.

"We caught her in the act of adultery," said one of her escorts. "The law of Moses says she needs to die. What do you say about her?"

Jesus bent down to write something on the ground. As he stood to face the crowd, the people became silent, waiting, wondering if he would agree with the sentence. And then he said, "He who is without sin among you, let him be the first to throw a stone at her."

Silently, he stooped down and continued writing on the ground with his finger. One by one the people turned and walked away, the older ones first. Soon the only people left there were Jesus and the woman.

"Woman," he said to her gently, "where are they? Did no one condemn you?"

The woman probably looked around at the spot where dozens of people had once stood. Still trembling over the thought of a painful and degrading death, she looked around and saw that everyone had gone. "No one, Lord."

And Jesus said, "Neither do I condemn you; go your way. From now on, sin no more." We can imagine the joy and relief of this woman as she went on her way (see Jn 8:1-11).

Though stoning is no longer a means of execution in our culture, there are many people who are stoning their self-images with guilt. The sin may not have been adultery but any number of other offenses against God. Jesus told the woman that he did not condemn her. Neither does he condemn us when we obey his words to "go and sin no more."

We don't really know if this woman went on to lead a completely moral life, but this is implied. She may even have gone on to be a close follower of Jesus. We can learn from her. Perhaps you have obeyed the words of Christ and are "sinning no more." But if you still feel condemned, you are bound by guilt and low self-esteem. Though some people around you may still be holding stones regarding the sin of your past, Jesus does not. And he's the one who counts. Go, and have guilt no more.

WORDS TO CONSIDER

There are many scriptural words of encouragement to those who have had their self-worth damaged. Here are a few that might be helpful for meditation.

When you feel like a failure. "I can do all things through him who strengthens me" (Phil 4:13).

"Not that we are adequate in ourselves to consider anything as coming from ourselves, but our adequacy is from God, who also made us adequate as servants of a new covenant, not of the letter, but of the Spirit; for the letter kills, but the Spirit gives life" (2 Cor 3:5-6).

When you feel weak and worthless. "And you have come to fullness in him, who is the head of every ruler and authority" (Col 2:10).

"[The Lord] said to me, 'My grace is sufficient for you, for my power is made perfect in weakness.' Therefore I will boast all the more gladly about my weaknesses, so that Christ's power may rest on me. That is why, for Christ's sake, I delight in weaknesses, in insults, in hardships, in persecutions, in difficulties. For when I am weak, then I am strong" (2 Cor 12:9-10).

When you feel alone and unloved. "As the Father has loved me, so I have loved you. Now remain in my love" (Jn 15:9).

"For I am convinced that neither death nor life, neither angels nor demons, neither the present nor the future, nor any powers, neither height nor depth, nor anything else in all creation, will be able to separate us from the love of God that is in Christ Jesus our Lord" (Rom 8:28-29).

When you can't forgive yourself. "God made him who had no sin to be sin for us, so that in him we might become the righteousness of God" (2 Cor 5:21).

"Therefore, there is now no condemnation for those who are in Christ Jesus" (Rom 8:1).

When you don't feel special. "For it was you who formed my inward parts; you knit me together in my mother's womb. I praise you for I am fearfully and wonderfully made. Wonderful are your works; that I know very well" (Ps 139:13-14).

When you feel unattractive. "For the Lord does not see as mortals see; they look on the outward appearance, but the Lord looks at the heart" (1 Sm 16:7).

When you feel without purpose. "For we are God's workmanship, created in Christ Jesus to do good works, which God prepared in advance for us to do" (Eph 2:10).

THE EMERGING BUTTERFLY

Changing the way we think about ourselves is not an easy process, nor does it happen overnight. But we *can* change. People who once saw themselves as worthless, ugly menaces to society have gone through an emotional and spiritual metamorphosis and have emerged as confident, loving, and self-respecting individuals. I've seen it happen in many of those around me, and I've seen a great deal of change in myself throughout the years. But unlike the butterfly who emerges from its cocoon by natural instinct, we must make a conscious decision to change the way we relate to the hurts of the past, our actions for today, and our relationship with God.

Since the transformation of a self-image is an ongoing process, there is no "quick-fix" method to change the way we feel about ourselves. However, the following steps provide a launching pad for you to use in analyzing the way you feel about yourself and to help you begin the metamorphosis process in your own life.

Step One: Paint your portraits. Before you can begin to improve the way you view yourself, it will be helpful to review the events and factors that contributed to the creation of the person you are today. Try going through your life in five-year increments, and draw a picture of the significant events of that time.

Don't worry about creating a masterpiece. You may just want to use stick figures or circles to represent various people who were a part of your life at each stage. Or if you feel you have absolutely no artistic ability, you may just want to write a narrative that explains how the portrait would look. Try to remember the good and bad things that you think might have influenced the development of your current self-image. Use complete creativity, but consider the following elements:

- family members who were present
- friends who were significant
- events that are permanently etched in your mind
- places where you spent much of your time

- thoughts that went through your mind or phrases that remain in your memories

When you have finished all of your portraits, make a list of those events and qualities that you feel were helpful in creating positive self-esteem and a list of those items you feel influenced your self-esteem in a negative way. Here is an example of how one person's list might look.

Age	Positive Self-Worth Events/Words	Negative Self-Worth Events/Words
5	Being held by Mom and Dad	Sexual abuse from Uncle Blake
10	Grandma telling me I'm pretty	Dad's drinking
15	Accepting Christ	Being called "Fatso"
20	Being accepted into the sorority	Sleeping around alot
25	Marrying Timothy	My continued weight problem
30		Tim's drinking and affair

On the one hand, the person just described might seem to have it all: parents who held her as a child, relatives who told her she was pretty, a relationship with Christ, social activities in college, and a marriage in her mid-twenties. But most likely the factors of the right side of this chart were more influential in the creation of her self-image.

Perhaps this first step does not appear to be one that will help to rebuild your poor self-worth. But suppressing and hiding the hurts of the past will do nothing more than cause further self-defeat. We must first seek to find where the problem lies and where the dirt is hiding. For example, we might think that the low self-esteem of the imaginary woman described above began with the cruel name-calling. But the name-calling was a result of the weight gain, and the weight gain may have been caused by the sexual abuse. One by one, we must examine our own portraits and try to heal the hurt they've created.

Step Two: Begin the forgiveness process. In the last chapter we discussed the process of forgiving others in your life. It is important to the strengthening of your own self-worth that you forgive those who helped to weaken it in the first place. This is especially true for those who have suffered physical, emotional, or sexual abuse.

But beyond the forgiveness of others, you must start the process of forgiving yourself. The woman in the example above may still feel unworthy because of her sexual promiscuity in college. Lisa, in our opening story, is still filled with shame from the abortion she had in high school. Follow the steps presented at the end of the previous chapter, but apply them to forgiving yourself rather than others.

Begin by focusing on the forgiveness of God. If he has forgiven you for the sins of your past, why do you continue to beat yourself up? It seems that we sometimes agonize and grieve over the things we've done so that God will know how sorry we are. But he doesn't need that kind of help from us. The grace we discussed in chapter two is sufficient for us. Let go of the things you did in the past. You are a new creature; the old has passed.

Step Three: Focus on the love of Jesus Christ. As long as we focus upon ourselves, we will probably never be able to truly achieve high self-esteem. There are people who do not worship God who appear to have a great deal of self-confidence and a high regard for themselves. But as we mentioned earlier in the chapter, high self-esteem is not to be confused with a strong ego. We will not find self-love by looking inward. Jesus doesn't love us because we are good; he loves us because *he* is good.

Focusing on Jesus is the primary and most important of all these steps to building our self-esteem. For as Christians, we find our self-worth in the love and grace of our Lord Jesus Christ. No matter how many names we are called, no matter how fat, goofy, or bald we look, no matter how many times we've failed, we are the prized treasure of the God who created us.

Close your eyes for a moment and picture yourself in a warm, cheerful room where Jesus is sitting. Picture yourself as a little boy or girl (or even as you are today) and walk over to Jesus. Imagine him picking you up, holding you, and filling you with thoughts of being his most valued treasure. He isn't mad about anything you've done. Nor does he condemn you for the times you've failed him. He loves you unconditionally, exactly as you are.

Allow yourself to create these and other comforting images and use them during times when your self-esteem is threatened or vulnerable. No words I or any other author could write would do a thimble-full of justice in describing the sea of love God has for each of us individually. It's only through images like the one I've just described that I can come somewhat in touch with the overwhelming love and acceptance Jesus Christ has for me. The only way to healthy self-esteem is to move the focus from ourself to the love of Father God, who knit each of us individually inside our mothers' womb.

Step Four: Change your views. A transformation of your self-worth may require an ongoing process of change in your life. You may need to break the patterns of thought that encroach upon your self-esteem. Perhaps you tend to compare what you have to what others have. Or you look in the mirror and see someone who isn't as attractive as you'd like to be. Or you tend to focus on all the areas where you come up short. Here are some things you might need to change as you continue to grow in self-worth.

Change your definition of success. We get ourselves into a great deal of trouble when we define success according to the world's definition. This leads to nothing but disaster. For in most cases, once we've achieved the next step on the ladder of success, there's another one right above it. There's always someone who is richer, better looking, thinner, has a bigger house, drives a nicer car, gets more dates, gets better grades, knows more people, raises smarter children, and so on. No wonder our self-worth is affected when we look at worldly success.

Jack Lemmon starred in a movie many years ago called *Save the Tiger.* Lemmon plays Harry, a top executive of a garment company who is caught up in striving for worldly success. He tries to juggle his business, big house, expensive tastes, bills, debts, and everything else until he is close to complete breakdown. He even hires an arsonist to burn down one of his factories in order to collect the insurance money.

Near the end of the movie Harry has a conversation with an old man named Meyer who has worked faithfully as his garment cutter. Harry says to Meyer something like, "You've worked all these years and what have you got? Nothing." And the old man replies something like, "I have my craft, my work, and my woman. She's old. But I love to hear her talk." What a contrast of success stories!

Nice homes, executive jobs, and high incomes are not in themselves wrong. But it is how we view these things that is important. If your self-worth is tied up in wealth and power rather than in love and contentment, you are striving for a worldly success that may not only get the best of your self-worth, it may destroy the very things you're trying to achieve. Are you seeking success in things or are you seeking God?

Change your appearance. If some of your low self-esteem is the result of your appearance, perhaps there is something you can do to change it. Even though we worship a God who loves us just as we are, I also believe that he is a God who wants us to take care of ourselves. One of the biggest changes in someone who has lost a great deal of weight is not their new wardrobe, but their new self-worth.

Some Christians would fault those who obtain plastic surgery to change a facial feature that has been disfigured. I recently read an article about a team of doctors who go throughout the world performing plastic surgery on children in poor countries so that they have a better chance of growing up with a normal lifestyle and stronger self-esteem. I applaud such heroes.

And I too applaud those who go through life as the not very attractive people who can do nothing to change the way they look—yet find themselves high in the self-esteem that comes from the love of God. I am one who tries to dress nicely, stay well-groomed, and keep my weight under control. But oh, how I wish I had a full head of hair! As Gilda Radner used to say, "It's always somethin'." And even though I wish I still had lots of blond hair, I try not to let the receding hair-line affect how I feel about myself. Looking the best I can with what I've got is important to me and my self-esteem.

Change the way you view your qualities. As you begin to build or continue building your self-esteem, make a list of all the positive qualities you see in yourself. Add to this list whenever a new quality comes to mind. In some cases, these may be the very qualities that once damaged your self-esteem.

For example, in my teenage and early adult years I was subject to quite a bit of teasing due to the fact that I was more sentimental and sensitive than most guys. You may know the type. My eyes tend to tear up during those sentimental long-distance telephone ads. You don't even want to be in the same room with me when an animal dies in a movie. For years I was ashamed of this quality, but now I cherish that part of me. In fact, as a pastor I am grateful now that God has given me a heart that is moved by the pain of the world.

In the space below or on a separate piece of paper, make a list of your good qualities. See if you too might have a few that used to negatively affect your self-worth but that are part of your uniqueness. Save this list and add to it as time goes on.

My Positive Traits

_____

_____

_____

_____

_____

_____

Change your actions. This step may be one of the most difficult of all because it may force you to break some patterns that have been around for a long time. It may force you to move away from some relationships that seem important but that tear away at your self-esteem as you try to rebuild. It may force you into a completely new way of thinking about the comments of others.

If your self-worth was affected because one or both of your parents was abusive or addicted to drugs or alcohol, there is a strong possibility that you could get caught up in the same behavior as you raise your children. Stop the cycle and get help now.

If you were raised by perfectionist parents, realize that perfection is not only unreasonable, it is impossible. Allow yourself to fail at some things. Perhaps you might even be able to laugh at some project you attempted that turned out less than perfect. If you usually are disappointed at work that is ninety percent right, lower your standards to striving for eighty percent work. Then you'll usually exceed your expectations rather than fall short of them.

We talked earlier about the fact that singleness sometimes affects people's self-worth. Rather than focusing on all of the reasons why you think you are *not* married, try focusing upon ways you can enjoy your life as a single person—no matter what your age or circumstance. Spend time with the people you love. Develop your interests. Serve the church and the needy. Enjoy the uniqueness God has given you. Think of alternatives to avoid pain. If Christmas shopping alone is depressing, find some friends to go along and make it an enjoyable experience.

It is also important to guard our minds from negative talk. One of the secrets of life is being able to accept the criticism and suggestions of others, but another secret is knowing when to ignore their comments as simply untrue. Knowing what to accept and what to ignore is a skill that becomes keener as we grow in our God-centered self-esteem.

To avoid further hurt to your self-image, you may have to terminate certain friendships that do nothing but tear you apart personally. Perhaps there is someone in your life whom you love deeply but who doesn't love you. Whenever you're around them you feel worthless and take their lack of love personally. Or perhaps your boss is emotionally abusive. You may need to find another job, even a lower-paying one, to avoid further humiliation. Part of our growth in the search for self-worth comes in our not allowing hurtful people to control us.

Lisa's self-worth was affected by an abortion when she was sixteen. Toby was neglected as a little boy and for years searched for what he'd missed out on. We all face similar pains in the years that have passed since our birth. And whether we're looking for the lost child, the missing father, or anything else, there is one place where we can find total, unqualified love and self-acceptance. That is in the loving arms of our Lord Jesus Christ. Seek help. Seek change. But most of all, seek him.

* FIVE *

Who's in Control?

* * *

Facing Our Dependencies

No one can serve two masters; for either he will hate the one and love the other, or he will hold to one and despise the other. You cannot serve God and mammon.   **Mt 6:24 NAS**

Habits that Hurt

Serving mammon
Dependent relationships
Controlling other people
Clinging to dependencies

Symptoms

Denying problems
Ignoring advice
Manipulating Scripture
Losing relationships
Changing personality traits

Habits that Heal

Depending on God
Seeking professional help
Treating others with kindness
Staying accountable to others

* * *

TED AND MAGGIE HAD BEEN MARRIED for over twenty-five years. While their first years together had been happy, the last few had been shaky at best.

Maggie had built a very successful interior design company and become nationally known for her work. She spent a great deal of time at her office and traveled extensively throughout the world. Although success had been good to her financially, it was slowly destroying every part of her life. And she didn't even see it happening.

A few years ago, Maggie achieved her goal of making over $100,000 in one year. But that goal had long since slipped her memory, for this year she was hoping to hit the $200,000 mark. The more money she made, the more she wanted.

The only friends Maggie had time for were the ones who could provide her a way to make more money or to achieve more power in the design business. The turnover within her company was high because staff people were intimidated by her insistence on controlling everything and everyone. She was rude to employees in staff meetings. She often made designers redo their work just to let them know she was in charge.

Maggie's need for power and control extended beyond her business. She became like a runaway train, focusing only on her desire to make more money and control everything within her reach. Her two children, Kevin and Kris, now away at college, wanted nothing to do with her. They were tired of her trying to control their every move. Everything in the household revolved around what Maggie wanted. Ted had been cut from his job in the defense industry. As weeks of unemployment turned into months, Ted fell into a deep depression. One day he opened his Bible, hoping to find some answers to his situation. At first he used the Bible in a healthy way, particularly finding comfort in the Psalms of David. Before long, however, he used his Bible reading as an excuse not to look for work, as a means of escaping from Maggie, and as a way to ignore his situation. The Scriptures became like an anesthetic drug for Ted as he sought to dull all the pain from his life.

Kevin and Kris were driven even further away—this time from their father. No longer could they have a heart-to-heart talk with this man to whom they had once been so close. Every question they asked was answered with a sermon, complete with chapter and verse references. When they needed a listening ear or hug of affirmation, Ted would get out his concordances to analyze all of the Scriptures relating to their problem. Forgetting that Christ died for sinners, he told his kids that they would burn in hell if they didn't turn completely away from sin. Worst of all, he gave his own interpretations to Scripture, often using them to condemn their mother's behavior.

Maggie and Ted were strangers to one another. She was controlled by her need for money and power; he had lost touch with all relationships, including his relationship with God, because of a religious addiction.

NO ONE IS IMMUNE

Twenty or thirty years ago, few people talked publicly about addictions and dependencies. As time moved on, famous actors, first ladies, and sports figures began to tell their stories of the fight against dependency upon various substances. Today, in addition to the more recognizable dependencies upon alcohol and drugs, health care professionals treat people who are dealing with a wide variety of issues. Some of the most commonly treated ones include:

- the need to have power over others
- compulsive sexual behaviors
- perfectionism
- out-of-control spending
- compulsive gambling
- codependency
- religion as an escape
- compulsive overeating

- relationship dependencies
- eating disorders
- workaholism

In my previous work as an executive with a Christian in-patient treatment program, part of my job was to meet with pastors of churches in areas where the treatment centers were located. When talking about a need for caring, in-patient treatment in the Christian community, I was always amazed at how many pastors would say, "We would never have need for those kind of services. No one in my church has problems with dependencies. My people love the Lord." Or, "We don't have people in our church who get depressed or suicidal. If someone seems a little down, I just refer them to our prayer committee. I know they're in good hands there."

Perhaps you question why a book directed at the Christian community would address the problems of dependencies. Unfortunately, people facing these problems can be found in every church. The church and Christian organizations recently have been particularly vulnerable to people who are controlled by things such as the love of money, the need for power, and sexual misconduct.

Fortunately, we Christians have the best resource for healing from such afflictions—the miraculous power and forgiveness of our Lord Jesus Christ. *That's* how we differ from the rest of society.

Because of the limited scope of this chapter, we will examine dependencies very generally and provide illustrations of some common problems. There are a number of very good resources available that focus on substance abuse and other addictions that affect even those of us in God's kingdom. For a good overview I would recommend a book entitled *Healing Life's Hidden Addictions*, written by Dr. Archibald Hart.

WHAT IS A DEPENDENCY?

Every dependency takes us further away from our relationship with God. The more progressive the dependency on other things becomes, the less we depend upon him. Some people allow a controlling substance or behavior to completely replace their relationship with Christ.

Generally, behaviors become dependencies when we cannot control them any more. We continue with these behaviors in spite of the harmful consequences. Most people become dependent upon behaviors because the process provides some nurturing or covers up voids or negative feelings within. While a healthy person may reach out to God, family, and friends for intimate support, the dependent person turns to power, sex, food, money, or any number of other things for solace. Such people fall into thinking that God and others have let them down but they can always trust the thing upon which they depend. People like Maggie who seek power over everyone around them may sincerely believe that they have lots of friends because of all the people they see daily. In reality they are very lonely people. Most dependencies lead to isolation and loneliness.

Dependency is progressive in nature and may come out of a harmless simple activity. As the dependency process begins, the dependent behavior becomes just as satisfying as the "high" obtained by some people through the use of alcohol or drugs. The behavior often leads to dangerous or even destructive consequences. In the final stages, the dependency becomes the singular focus of the person's life. This is why it is so harmful to our spiritual walk. God is the focus of a Christian's life, and he is the only one on whom we can depend.

Maggie experienced this progression in her drive to succeed. She started with a small interior design firm with two people on the payroll. Once she landed her first major hotel job, Maggie felt the adrenaline rush from the excitement. So she sought bigger deals that would bring her more money, more fame, more control—and most of all that same great feeling.

Each person's dependency problem is unique. While physicians, psychologists, and other mental health workers seem to disagree on the specific causes or personality traits that result in such disorders, it is clear that in evaluating the cause and treatment, professionals must look at the physiological, psychological, and spiritual make-up of the person. Treating one of these aspects without considering the others may place a "band-aid" on the problem, but will probably not result in life-long change and recovery.

Some people are fortunate in that they go through life with very few dependencies. Others seem to be compulsive and addictive by nature. There are committed Christian men and women in both of these groups. The goal of this chapter is to confront the areas of our lives where we need help in order to begin controlling the things that control us.

CHARACTERISTICS OF DEPENDENCY

People who have allowed money, power, or any other item to control their lives have many of the same characteristics as those who become addicted to drugs, alcohol, or sex. The following are common factors present in those who take things to excess.

Denial: the greatest roadblock to recovery. There are people who walk through life with the serious problems we are discussing, yet who are unwilling to face the fact that they need help. And it doesn't make it any easier that those closest to them also deny the problem by making excuses for their actions. Denial is in itself a symptom of dependency.

Denial of a dependency problem is expressed in many ways. One tactic the dependent person uses is to compare himself with others. Someone who is dependent on power over others may say, "You should go to work for our competitor. Their president makes me look like Santa Claus." We can always seem to find someone who is more dependent upon something than we are. Yet this is no excuse for our behavior.

We also deny our problems by highlighting other areas of our lives that appear to be successful. Maggie may feel that her controlling actions are justified by how successful her business is. The anorexic may use her figure to show how successful she can be in maintaining a body without fat. She may think her ability to control her weight is admirable, but food actually has control over her.

Pointing the finger at others is another method of denial. Do you know someone who is always talking about how emotionally unstable everyone else is? "Can you believe how irrational she is? Must have had a horrible childhood to be that insecure." "I think he should seek psychiatric help. I heard he grew up in a very dysfunctional family. No wonder he argues with everything I say. He just can't submit to authority." If you are always finding fault with everyone else when your friendships or other relationships don't work out, consider looking at the things that control you, rather than the things you see wrong in the reactions of others.

The purpose of this book is to help you address the habits that hurt in your own life. Jesus gives very clear instructions as to what we are to do when confronting problems we see in one another (see Mt 18:15-20). As you read parts of this chapter, the dependencies in others may come to mind. But remember that you are included when Paul says that "all have sinned and fall short of the glory of God" (Rom 3:23). In Galatians 6:1 he further says, "Brothers, if someone is caught in a sin, you who are spiritual should restore him gently. But watch yourself, or you also may be tempted." Before you shake your head at the sin in other peoples' lives, look first at the sin within your own life. We can also deny a dependency problem by creating our own definitions of what a dependency is. One who is controlled by the love of money may give five percent of her income to charity. "How can you say that I'm greedy?" she may ask. The "social drinker" who performs well on the job may think that an alcoholic is someone who misses work frequently because he is always drunk. So he justifies his three drinks each night as uncharacteristic of the type of alcoholic he has created in his mind. He sincerely believes that he has no problem with alcohol.

Family and friends of the dependent person have their own denial problems. Often they want help for their loved ones on the one hand, but they make excuses for the person on the other. Some make excuses to protect their loved ones from ridicule or harm. Others simply think that the person will eventually change and suddenly be free from the problem. Still more fear that the abuser is behaving in such a way because of something they've done. Ted was driven to his religious excess by his desire to escape from his poor relationship with Maggie. But being in denial, Maggie did not see her behavior as a contributing factor.

Relationship problems. People who are controlled by their need for more money, more power, or more fame are most likely offending the people closest to them. As the need increases, the importance of relationships seems to decline.

Soon the greedy or controlled person uses even his friends for his own gain—financial or otherwise. The attention gained by being well-known in their profession becomes just like an addictive drug: the more attention they get, the more they want. This is very common among popular pastors and others in the Christian public eye.

Meanwhile, the spouse and children feel left out. Friends would rather not spend time with the person, and the people at work begin to see him as a villain. One day the successful, wealthy, famous person turns around, and there is no one there. If the cycle continues, he will say it's because everyone was jealous of his success.

In virtually all types of dependencies, relationships suffer because of the distrust, suspicion, and anger that begin to build. As the abuser's habits get worse and worse, so do his relationships. The addicted person begins telling small lies to cover up his behavior. Soon the small lies turn into big lies. The concerned spouse, child, or friend eventually finds out. Relationships shatter, and families fall apart. Despite all of this relational disaster, many abusers still don't get help. The controlling desire is more important to them than the people they hurt.

Personality or behavior changes. Sure signs of a progressing dependency are changes in personality or behavior.

If you are a parent and you begin to notice things such as your child's grades dropping, more radical clothing, or a new set of friends, there may be a chance your child has become involved in the use of an addictive substance.

Many of the examples in this chapter reflect various personality alterations. If you are in denial of your problems, you may not even notice the change in your own behavior, but others around you surely will. The following changes in behavior are common as someone becomes engulfed in a dependency.

- *Increased anger.* Little things seem to set you off. Your anger is misdirected at people who did nothing to hurt you.
- *Less need for God.* All dependencies interfere with our spiritual lives. As one seeks more power, more fame, or more romantic encounters, God moves further down the priority list.
- *Deterioration of self-image.* Your ongoing activity or dependency may slowly be chipping away at your self-worth. As shame increases, you think less and less of yourself.
- *Depression.* You no longer just have the blues. More days than not you are filled with feelings of loneliness, grief, and negative thoughts.
- *Altered personality.* You find yourself acting like another person. Sometimes you say things you normally wouldn't say. You may even regress into a behavior more indicative of a child. Where you once were an extrovert, you now find yourself very introverted—or vice versa.

A loss of or distorted perspective. Jennifer was going to a formal fund-raiser with Darren, a man at church she had been interested in for a very long time. She was certain that this was her big chance to fall in love and join the "in" crowd in one packaged deal. Jennifer's finances were in trouble. Her car had been repossessed, most of her credit cards had been canceled, and her landlady had given her an eviction notice. None of her friends knew anything about her financial state. With the look of success, she was living a lie.

Jennifer knew that the upcoming date was the event that would change her life. So she took her one remaining credit card and purchased the most beautiful dress she'd ever seen. At the night of the big event, everyone complimented her stunning appearance. She even sensed that Darren was proud to be with her. Weeks later Jennifer got a notice from the department store that the dress had put her over the limit. And due to her poor payment record, their card would also be canceled. Darren hadn't called her since the night of the event. So Jennifer, in a state of despair, headed for the mall. Buying some things she needed would surely keep her mind off the pain.

Several months ago I tore an article out of a popular newspaper regarding one of the nation's wealthiest men. It seems that he found his two hundred eighty-two foot yacht, which had been listed by the *Guinness Book of World Records* as the longest private yacht in the world, was too small for his needs. His new ship would be four hundred twenty feet and have a crew of almost fifty.

Since I don't know the man personally, I can't say that he has a distorted perspective on life. But having been on yachts that seemed incredibly spacious at eighty feet, I find it almost incomprehensible that a two hundred eighty-two footer would be inadequate. On a much smaller scale, there are people who always want more when they live quite comfortably. There are people like Jennifer who spend money beyond their means just to be accepted by a certain class of individuals.

There are people who lack perspective with a problem completely opposite of Jennifer's. In the early twentieth century the world's richest woman had no problem in being able to afford the best clothes. Yet year after year she wore the same black dress. Although she had inherited a great deal of money and made a killing on Wall Street, she still sat in her office clipping coupons. She ate in inexpensive restaurants and left no tips. Worth millions, she would argue over the price of some sundry at the pharmacy.

The woman had every right to be eccentric with her lack of spending; after all, it was her money. It is told that she was very helpful to others as long as it didn't involve money. But her lack of perspective literally cost her son his leg. Dressed in rags, she went to a doctor to see if he would provide free services for her son's knee, which had been injured months before but had never healed. When the doctor realized the woman had money, he demanded payment and she quickly left the office. Some time later her son's leg had to be amputated because it was never cared for.

People caught up in compulsive or controlling behaviors are very often out of touch with the reality of their situation. Jennifer's canceled credit card notices should have been enough of a warning to her. Yet even when she hit rock bottom, her solution was to head for the mall.

Have you lost perspective on certain areas of your life? Do you commit to too many activities? Do you feel that the things you have are not adequate when, in reality, you live far beyond most people's dreams? Or like the wealthy woman, do you keep others, even those you love, from getting help because it might cost you money?

Excessive paranoia or worry. If you are caught up in dependency, you probably experience times of great worry or paranoia. The one who drinks or uses drugs might have thoughts such as, "What did I do last night? I was so drunk I can't remember." The person who is active in some sexual addiction may think, "What if someone saw me coming out of his apartment? They're going to tell my pastor. I'll lose my job. My life will be ruined." If you worry about your behavior but feel powerless to change it, you may be caught in the trap of dependency.

Manipulation of Scripture. Jeremy had just become an elder at the church. A good-looking man, Jeremy was the football coach at the local high school. Many of the women in his small town were attracted to him. Despite his strong commitment to the church, Jeremy had a very active sexual life, sometimes sleeping with three or four different women in one weekend. In fact, his last marriage was destroyed by his infidelity. Although he tried to put all of that behind him when he moved to a new state and joined a new church three years ago, his old patterns seemed to follow.

Michael, one of his fellow elders, became aware of Jeremy's lifestyle after his sister became one of Jeremy's partners. When Michael decided to confront Jeremy regarding his role as an elder and his commitment to be "above reproach," Jeremy rationalized his behavior. He told Michael that he only had sex with women he loved.

"Most of the Bible was written two thousand or more years ago. Times have changed," he said. "Sex may have been reserved for married people then, but this is another culture. I have no problem with how I live my life. I'm a committed Christian. I have a heart for God, and I never do anything to hurt people. I only sleep with women who want me to. This is the nineties, not the first century."

Rationalization is common for those who are facing dependencies; Christians add the problem of manipulating or misinterpreting Scripture. There are a great many Christian people who take the Word of God and change the literal meaning in order to justify their bad habit or continued sin. What is even sadder, many people in the church would excuse someone like Jeremy because he was squeaky clean in all other areas of his life. "A guy that good-looking? I'd have trouble resisting all of those beautiful women too. After all, this is the nineties."

A singular focus. Leonard became a Christian as part of the high school group in his church. From the day he entered college, he knew that he wanted to be a pastor. While attending a Christian college, Leonard met his wife Colleen. After graduation he entered a well-respected seminary, while Colleen worked in the admissions department. After four years Leonard graduated and was assigned a small church in the suburbs of Dallas. Everything seemed to be going so well during his first year at Community Church. Colleen even gave birth to twins.

During the next few years, however, problems developed. Leonard left very early each morning and returned home after the twins were fed, bathed, and in bed. Even on Saturday, Leonard would be at the church working on his sermon. Sundays after church he did most of his hospital visitations.

On the outside it appeared that Leonard was the ideal pastor: leading Bible studies throughout the week, visiting people on weekends, and doing things for just about everyone—everyone, that is, except Colleen, the twins, and himself. Leonard sincerely felt that he was serving God to the best of his ability. In reality, Leonard didn't even know who God was anymore. His ministry had become a routine, not a relationship. His sermons had Scripture but lacked sensitivity. His visitations and leadership responsibilities were motivated by compulsions rather than compassion.

This singular focus is common regardless of the dependency. Some alcoholics reach the point where nothing matters except the next drink. Many of those addicted to cocaine lose everything—home, children, job, savings—to continue with their habit. Those controlled by financial success will stop at nothing or will hurt anyone around them if it means making another dollar. If your life is becoming more and more focused on one issue, it's time that you take a good hard look at your situation and break from your denial now.

CONFRONTING AND
CONQUERING DEPENDENCY

Even those closest to Jesus established dependencies on things other than him. For thirty pieces of silver, Judas turned the Son of God over to his crucifiers. If money, power, sex, or some other item has taken priority over your love for him, Jesus Christ not only promises to restore you, but he'll bring you closer to him than ever before.

Recovery from dependencies is not an easy process. I'm sure there are those who have quit various compulsive bad habits "cold turkey." Many people are able to quit smoking one day and never return to it. Part of the struggle is getting over the addiction to the nicotine in the body, but breaking the habit of touching the cigarette to the lips is part of the psychological recovery. Some chew gum, eat sunflower seeds, or munch on a piece of licorice to replace that habit.

So while some habits can be stopped suddenly, we must remember that most dependencies have physical, psychological, and spiritual components. In addition to breaking the physical action or stopping the mental processes, recovery almost always involves an evaluation of the inner factors that caused the out-of-control behavior. We also must turn the problem over to God after we admit we cannot get through it alone.

There's a method often used in the recovery process to confront someone who is seriously addicted or under the control of something. This process is called intervention. All the people close to the addicted person meet together and invite the person into a room where each tells how much they love the person but also how much their behavior has caused them to be hurt. But the primary goal of this book is not to help you bring others to a confrontation with their problems, although it is an appropriate secondary goal. The primary purpose is for *you* to break out of the cycle of *your* dependencies.

If some issues have been raised as a result of your reading this chapter, use the following steps as guidelines to begin your process of turning from a life marred by dependency and starting on the road to a closer and better relationship with Jesus Christ.

Step One: Evaluate the things that control you. Consider for a moment all of the things in your life that you feel may be moving you further from God. Make a list in the space below or on a separate sheet of paper. Consider the ongoing things in your life that take you further away from God—things like workaholism, sexual promiscuity, the love of money, the need for power, the various things you do compulsively. But consider also those isolated incidents, the one-time mistakes you've made over the past one or two years that you fear may happen again: that one-night stand, the marijuana you smoked just because you were with old friends, the lie you told to hide something you were not proud of.

After you have made your list, evaluate the seriousness of each item. If you think an item was an isolated incident or behavior and that you sincerely have no problem in controlling it, give it a ranking of "1." If you see a negative behavior or thought increasing and think that you may be in danger of facing a dependency presently or someday, perhaps you'll give it a ranking of "5." If you are convinced that some area of your life is completely out of control, give that behavior a "10." For this exercise to be of any value to you, the first thing you must do is break out of denial. Consider how others would rank you. If you deny that you have a problem with greed, you might give yourself a "3" ranking, whereas most people you know would give you a "9" in that area. Do your best to rank yourself as others close to you would.

My Behavior

Personal Ranking

_____ _____

_____ _____

_____ _____

_____ _____

_____ _____

_____ _____

_____ _____

_____ _____

Consider the following questions with regard to your list. Since each reader may be dealing with different dependency behaviors, the questions will generically include all these issues by referring to "my behavior." If you are dealing with sexual issues (or know you are a sex addict), for example, replace the words "my behavior" with "my sexual activity." If your issue is money, insert the words "my love for money," and so on.

- Do I sometimes forget events revolving around my participation in my behavior?
- Am I often filled with guilt because of my behavior?
- Do I often have feelings of great regret because of my behavior?
- Have I hurt others I love because of my behavior?
- Has my behavior led me into any kind of problem with the law?
- Has my behavior led me into unethical practices?
- Does my behavior sometimes make me feel totally out of control?

- Have others confronted me on my behavior?
- Have I denied that my behavior is a problem when others approach me?
- Have I justified my behavior by manipulating Scripture?
- Has my behavior resulted in any kind of financial losses?
- Has the frequency of my behavior increased?
- Does my behavior interfere with my life in Christ?
- Does my behavior interfere with my time with family or friends?
- Does my behavior ever make me depressed or suicidal?
- Do other members of my family have problems similar to my behavior?
- Are there certain events that trigger my behavior?
- Do I turn to my behavior when I need to relax?
- Do I turn to my behavior because I need some form of excitement?
- Have I ever wished that my behavior would go away—for good?

Let me make it clear that there are people who do not struggle with issues of dependencies. If you can't think of anything for this list, don't feel you have to create something. Instead, thank God that you are not facing the pain of the addictive cycle. Find tools in your life to continue with your tradition of freedom. And most of all, celebrate the relationship you have with Christ, for if you are free of any dependencies, it is very likely because of your strong relationship with him.

Step Two: Realize your sin. We already know that we all sin and fall short of the glory of God. Dependency itself is not always sin. Sometimes, however, a dependency causes the continued repetition of sinful behavior. Being an alcoholic is not a sin; drunkenness and avoidance of recovery is. Financial security is not a sin; the love of money and the drive for continued wealth at the expense of others or your faith is. Whether our addiction is caused by a physical dependence, psychological voids from childhood, or any other reason, we cannot use these things as excuses. We are called to face the fact that they cause us to sin. We must seek change.

Ephesians 2:12 says, "As for you, you were dead in your transgressions and sins, in which you used to live when you followed the ways of this world and of the ruler of the kingdom of the air, the spirit who is now at work in those who are disobedient." This passage provides at least three reasons why we sin: 1) unbelievers sin because they are not centered in Christ; 2) believers sin because of the world's enticements: we get involved with harmful unbelievers, we fall into old patterns, we participate in earthly things; 3) and we all sin because Satan has a powerful influence over the earth and provides opportunities for sin.

The lack of understanding regarding sin can keep us caught up in the cycle of dependency. Years ago the comedian Flip Wilson's most famous line became "the devil made me do it." Unfortunately, far too many Christians use Flip's line as an excuse for their sin. For recovery to begin, we must confess that *we* are the ones who have sinned. The "ruler of the kingdom of the air" may tempt us or lead us to worldly places that make it easy for us to sin, but God gave us the will to choose between right and wrong. The decision is ours.

David is considered one of the most godly people in the Bible, someone whose faith we can use as a model. But at times he allowed factors other than God to control him. His lustful desire controlled him when he slept with Bathsheba. And although he felt shame, his lack of self-control led to further problems: he caused the death of Bathsheba's husband to hide his sin.

God brought David back to a close relationship with him, once David realized his mistake and repented. Psalm 51 reflects David's sorrow for sin:

> "Have mercy on me, O God,
>   according to your unfailing love;
> according to your great compassion
>   blot out my transgressions.
> Wash away all my iniquity
>   and cleanse me from my sin."

> "For I know my transgressions,
>   and my sin is always before me.
> Against you, you only, have I sinned
>   and done what is evil in your sight,
> so that you are proved right when you speak
>   and justified when you judge.
> Surely I was sinful at birth,
>   sinful from the time my mother conceived me...."

> "Cleanse me with hyssop, and I will be clean;
>   wash me, and I will be whiter than snow.
> Let me hear joy and gladness;
>   let the bones you have crushed rejoice.
> Hide your face from my sins
>   and blot out all my iniquity.
> Create in me a clean heart, O God,
>   and renew a steadfast spirit within me."

Ps 51:1-2, 3-5, 7-10 NIV

David is just one illustration of someone who blew it, changed, asked for forgiveness, and was restored to an even better relationship with God. If you feel unworthy to serve God because of your dependency or sinful behavior, you too can have a second, third, fourth, or five hundredth chance to start again. You can be freed from the things that bind you and enter that stronger relationship with him.

Step Three: Face your problem today. If your list in Step One helped reveal some controlling things that you now want to control, do not delay another day to make a change. If you seek change as the result of guilt from a recent experience, that alone will probably not be enough of a motivation to change. Guilt is a part of the dependency cycle. While it may stop the addicted or controlled person from another immediate failing. soon the guilt will dissipate and the dependency again will take control. Then the cycle of guilt will begin again. As Christians, the best motivation for change is our sincere desire to become more of the person that Christ wants us to be—to move as close to him as possible.

Recently I watched a television talk show on addictions. One of the guests dealing with the problem said he had gone to his pastor for help. The pastor told him that if he really wanted to stop his compulsive sexual dependencies, then he should just stop. I'm afraid that all too many people think that ending dependent behavior is that easy. True, avoiding the addictive behavior is necessary, but willpower alone rarely provides a plan for recovery. Most people need to honestly acknowledge their problem and seek help from others. Most of all, we need to turn our problems over to God. He has the power to fix all of these things. Here are some steps to take as you begin your fight to overcome dependent behavior.

Take responsibility for your actions. Before you can recognize that you have a problem and seek help, you must break free from the denial. You must quit pointing fingers at Satan for making you do things you didn't want to do. You must quit using God's grace as an excuse for your behavior. You must quit blaming your parents for the problem because they didn't raise you quite right. Say to yourself, I have a problem with _____. I am not a bad person. I just need help. Today I will seek that help and begin the road to recovery.

Avoid tempting situations. Romans 12:2 says, "And do not be conformed to this world, but be transformed by the renewing of your mind, that you may prove what the will of God is, that which is good and acceptable and perfect." Your mind may need a lot of renewing to break from the habits of this world.

If you are addicted to pornography, don't drive through the part of town where the adult bookstores and theaters are located. If you are a recovering alcoholic, you may not be able to go to a baseball game with all the buddies you once drank beer with. If you are a compulsive overeater, avoid all-you-can-eat buffets. If you spend money excessively, put your credit cards away until you can gain control.

Make necessary changes. A new life sometimes will mean major changes. To start your recovery from cocaine addiction, you may have to say farewell to your girlfriend who refuses to confront hers. If you use a behavior or substance to relax, you will need to find something healthy to help you relax. If you use your addictive behavior or substance for excitement and pleasure, you will have to find something healthy that gives you pleasure. Instead of eating when you really aren't hungry, take a walk to the local park. Instead of working late to occupy your time, ask your wife out for a nice dinner. If you seek power over everyone, begin by attending a meeting and being passive and helpful rather than dominant and offensive.

Practice self-control. Self-control is something we must learn; it is a habit. The next two chapters provide suggestions for some behaviors and disciplines that might contribute to your ability to maintain more self-control.

The best principle for self-control is obedience to God. For obedience *always* leads to a blessed, peaceful, and fulfilling life. Disobedience *always* leads to sadness, sin, regret, shame, and even death. Titus 2:11-12 says, "For the grace of God that brings salvation has appeared to all men. It teaches us to say 'No' to ungodliness and worldly passions, and to live self-controlled, upright and godly lives in this present age." And 1 Peter 5:8 instructs us to "Be self-controlled and alert. Your enemy the devil prowls around like a roaring lion looking for someone to devour."

Give yourself a break. Some dependencies are centered around perfectionism. If keeping your house clean forces you to turn down social engagements or miss things you'd really like to do, allow yourself to have some dirty dishes in the sink once in a while. Perhaps you regularly drive twenty miles per hour over the speed limit on the freeway, even when you have all the time in the world. This makes you irritable toward other drivers. Try driving the speed limit in the slow lane as often as you can. If you are compulsively on time, realize that being ten minutes late is not the end of the world.

Step Four: Develop a healthy dependency upon God. There is one dependency that we were created for. That is the dependency upon the infinite love, wisdom, and forgiveness of God. God will *never* leave us.

As discussed earlier in this chapter, dependency on Christ should not be confused with an addiction to some type of service, ritual, or scriptural manipulation. Such practices can be termed "ianity"—taking Christ out of Christianity. We must seek Christ himself.

One of my favorite Scriptures is the last few words of the book of Matthew. Here the risen Lord gives his disciples the great commission. And he says to them, "I am with you *always,* even to the end of the age." After a great many years of searching I finally believed those words a few years ago. And the presence of Jesus Christ is with me wherever I go. It is my hope that if you currently are dependent on something, your dependency would shift to that of the love that God infinitely pours out upon you.

Search the Scriptures to learn more about God. Read them often. Perhaps you can start by reading Psalm 51, the words of David discussed earlier in this chapter. The book of Psalms is a great arena for those who wish to change habits that hurt and find comfort in doing so.

God's infinite grace is available to you. He accepts you and wants to set you free from your compulsions. His forgiveness washes you whiter than snow. And his love is so great that we cannot even understand it in human terms. God is not pointing the finger at your dependencies and shortcomings. He is reaching out his hand to pull you closer to himself.

Step Five: Seek professional help. Very few people can break the cycle of dependency on their own. And even though I have made this suggestion to seek help in other chapters, it is extremely relevant when confronting addictive behavior.

Depending on your need, there are several options. You may be able to begin your recovery through individual therapy with a qualified psychiatrist, psychologist, or licensed counselor. You may even need to spend two or three weeks in a qualified in-patient setting. Here you will be able to focus completely on the issues surrounding your dependency without the distraction of work, household chores, and the everyday grind of life.

Hundreds of thousands of people have been helped through regular participation in the various twelve-step recovery programs. These programs are offered for people dealing with alcohol dependencies, compulsive overeating, cocaine addiction, sexual addiction, compulsive gambling, and almost every other major dependency troubling people in our world today.

All of the above options are available in the Christian community. It will be important in your recovery that you not only address the physical addiction but also try to find out what you might be trying to cover up through the use of drugs, sex, food, power, or any other behavior. I've mentioned several times that stopping the behavior is only part of the issue. A piece of electrical tape may keep a plastic pipe from leaking for a while. But as the pressure rebuilds and the adhesive weakens, the water will burst forth again.

Seek help. Find out why you are searching for acceptance through extramarital affairs. Discover why you need alcohol or drugs to escape from the pain of your current situation or the hurts of your past. See if food has become your friend because you are trying to fill an empty place in your heart instead of an empty place in your stomach. With caring, qualified help you can break free from dependencies physically, emotionally, and spiritually.

Step Six: Build a support base and remain in it. Once you start on the road to recovery, you do not want to walk it alone. Even though we are to be dependent upon God and God alone, he often provides that comfort and support through other people.

I'm reminded of the story of the man whose boat sank at sea. As he tread water he began to pray, "O Lord, reach down your hand and save me from this sea."

Shortly thereafter a boat came by and spotted the drowning man. But when they threw a life preserver out to rescue him he responded, "Keep going. I'm waiting for God to save me." A little while later a helicopter flew by and dropped its harness. But again the man refused help, yelling up to the pilot, "Go ahead. I'm waiting for God to save me." Just then a great fish came up from beneath the man and began to carry him toward shore. But the man jumped off and finally drowned.

When he arrived in heaven the man asked why God's hand never came to save him. God said, "I sent you a boat. Then I sent you a helicopter. I even provided safety on the back of a great fish. I sent you lots of help. You just didn't see that it was from me."

How true to life this story can be. God has given us friends and a community of believers to provide support for us. When your brother is weak, perhaps you can be strong. When you are weak, your sister can be there to help you.

You may find this kind of support through a small group at church, through regular appointments with a very special friend, or through a twelve-step program. Recovery is not an independent journey. It requires the guidance of professionals, a dependence upon God, and the loving support of others. Begin your road to recovery today. If you always put it off till tomorrow, that tomorrow never comes.

SIX

Beyond
Sunday Morning

✳ ✳ ✳

Maintaining Christian Integrity

But the fruit of the Spirit is love, joy, peace,
patience, kindness, goodness, faithfulness,
gentleness, self-control;
against such things there is no law.

Gal 5:22-23 NAS

Habits that Hurt

Hiding our faith between Sunday mornings
Behaving as unbelievers
Overcontrolling our emotions
Lacking compassion

Symptoms

An uncontrolled tongue
Lack of integrity in the workplace
Poor financial accountability
Pride, bigotry, and jealousy

Habits that Heal

Exemplifying Christ in our words, actions, and deeds
Maintaining integrity in all walks of life
Illustrating the fruits of the Spirit
Expressing emotions in a healthy way

* * *

RECENTLY I READ AN ARTICLE about an arsonist who had set fire to over thirty churches in the state of Florida during 1991. All had been severely damaged or completely destroyed, totaling millions of dollars worth of damage. Although the perpetrator has not yet been captured, an arson authority suggested that the person probably is setting the fires out of revenge. Perhaps he was hurt by some church staff member. Maybe he became disillusioned because of some hypocritical Christian in his life. Or perhaps the arsonist's anger is directed at God himself.

Fortunately, even though this story is tragic, most of these churches have a good chance of survival. This is true because the church is *not* a set of buildings constructed for weekly worship. Rather, the church is the body of believers who meet with a common commitment and love for Jesus Christ.

CHURCHES IN PERIL

There are churches that face a far worse danger than that of arsonists who hold matches and gasoline cans. There are more insidious enemies within the church itself, armed with anger, strife, gossip, jealousy, envy, greed, deceit, arrogance, pride, and disobedience. These forces can destroy a Christian body, as well as inhibit evangelism. There are nonbelievers who simply reject the gospel; but I'm convinced there are at least as many nonbelievers who are unwilling to trust in Christ because the Christian people in their lives have completely turned them off. Instead of love, joy, and compassion, they have been exposed to hypocrisy, greed, judgmental quotes from Scripture, and all the other behaviors just mentioned.

In March the Christian corporation where Ivan worked had to make some cuts in their expenses because of a slow economy. Rather than cutting many people who were in the middle-salary level, the management decided it could save money by cutting a few higher paid people such as Ivan, who was a vice-president. December came and Ivan was still unemployed. With his house on the market, little funds left in his savings, and two children who were expecting Christmas gifts, he was not looking forward to the holiday season.

The company for whom Ivan had worked was now doing

extremely well. Ivan tried to have a good attitude as to why the company had to make some cuts. But when he heard that the remaining executives were to receive tens of thousands of dollars in year-end bonuses because of the company's third and fourth-quarter success, Ivan became disillusioned and vowed never to work for a Christian organization again.

Unfortunately, there are an awful lot of "Ivans" running around in our society—those who have worked for "Christian" organizations or who have been actively involved in a church only to be treated with less compassion, integrity, or purity than they would have in most secular organizations. When we get involved with a Christian organization or church, we expect more out of the people. And we should!

WHAT KIND OF FRUIT DO YOU BEAR?

This chapter is focused on our need to maintain integrity as Christians in all the roles we fill, whether in church, in the home, or in the workplace. In the following pages some basic guidelines will be presented for us to follow between Sunday mornings. These guidelines are not written to be sources of guilt. We already know that we are saved by grace, not by our works. Yet, our Lord created us to be in his likeness. And he sent the Holy Spirit to guide our lives. Galatians 5:22-23, printed at the beginning of this chapter, lists some of the fruit of the Spirit which should be evident in the lives of those filled with the love of God.

How do you act throughout the week? Examine all the roles you fill: as father or mother, son or daughter, husband or wife, brother or sister, friend, church member, employee, employer, Christian.

In any of these roles, do you operate according to the flesh? Are you prone to anger, strife, gossip, jealousy, envy, greed, deceit, arrogance, pride, disobedience, dissension, hypocrisy? Or do you reflect the fruit of the Spirit through your love, joy, patience, kindness, goodness, faithfulness, gentleness, and self-control?

These are the topics we will be discussing in this chapter. For even if we are able to make progress in changing the bad habits of doubt, unforgiveness, low self-esteem, and dependencies previously discussed, our spiritual life may still be greatly affected because the destructive works of the flesh block our further growth in Christ.

Not long ago I saw an educational program on television about a certain species of ant. Alone the tiny creatures seem insignificant. But this species travels in groups of millions. Their trail is miles long and about a foot wide. They destroy everything in their path. If a small waterway or hole blocks their way, they form a bridge using hundreds of their tiny little bodies. When an ant falls into the water below while serving as a part of the bridge, another can take its place. The film showed several thousand ants attack a very large lizard and virtually eat him alive.

So is it with the works of the flesh that creep into our path daily. Often the little things we do each day, when joined with other little things, can cause great destruction in our lives and sometimes in the churches or relationships of which we are a part.

Let's look now at the works of the flesh that chip away at our integrity as Christians. Some of these points may not be considered sinful, but they can be good indicators of how closely we walk with God. We'll examine some characteristics that might encroach on our integrity in relationships, in our personal lives, in the workplace, and in our church.

MAINTAINING CHRISTIAN INTEGRITY
IN OUR RELATIONSHIPS

Since our relationships with others are so integral to all areas of our lives, it would be helpful to start our discussion of Christian integrity here. Think about your role as a mother, husband, son, friend, or in any other personal relationship. Consider the following questions.

Do you spend regular, valuable time with loved ones? The most valuable thing we can give anyone we love is our time. As we will see in the next chapter, fellowship with others is one of the spiritual disciplines that supplements our individual time with God. Has your time with the closest people in your life—your spouse, best friends, children, parents, siblings, and others—become a low priority, almost a distraction to your busy schedule? Just as God honors the commitment we make to him, he expects us to keep the commitments we make to one another. How much time each week do you spend focused on the needs of those whom you love the most? How much more time should you be spending?

Do you keep promises? Although the old cliché says that "promises are made to be broken," those who practice this habit regularly are probably offending the people closest to them. How often have you promised to take your child somewhere only to cancel because of some emergency at work? Is there a project you promised to accomplish months ago that still hasn't been started? Have some people in your life lost trust in most things you say because you seldom keep your word?

Sometimes family members or close friends tell us things that they expect us to keep confidential. Except in rare cases where keeping their confidence would allow another person to be hurt wrongfully, we should always respect and honor their request for privacy and confidentiality.

Are you other-centered? In John 13, Jesus washed the feet of his disciples. When he had finished he said to them, "If I then, the Lord and the Teacher, washed your feet, you also ought to wash one another's feet" (v. 14). As a parent, child, spouse, or friend, Jesus calls us to minister to one another— to do for others rather than having them do for us. Here are just a few examples of how we can be servants to one another:

- listening to others more than talking to them
- learning to accept others rather than preaching why they should change
- putting the needs of others above our own
- placing ourselves in the shoes of others
- holding another's hand when their life seems unfair
- doing things for others without need for reward
- swallowing our pride and conquering the fear that prevents us from helping

Are you affirming? It has always amazed me that it is so easy for us to criticize and be angry with one another and so difficult for us to praise and affirm one another. This seems especially true for men. However, one of the fruits of the Spirit is kindness, another is goodness, still another is gentleness. What better way to show these qualities to one another than through regular praise and affirmation of those closest to us. We need to take more time to tell people we love them. We should send more cards, make more calls, and treat people as someone special each time we see them.

A close friend of mine recently died. Just before she did, I was able to hold her hand and tell her that I loved her. Ever since that day I've been saying these words to many other people I haven't told before. We should never take for granted the people in our lives. Life is so fragile that any one of the people in your life could be gone tomorrow. Spend your time with those you love as if it were their last day.

Do you show loyalty in each relationship? Nothing destroys a relationship like a lack of loyalty. Think of how Jesus felt when Judas turned him over to the authorities. What pain Christ must have felt to see one of those he had chosen turn his back on him. Unfortunately, many in the Christian community still betray the people they love. Husbands are unfaithful to their wives. Friends turn their backs on one another. Daughters hate their fathers.

Consider how often you say negative things about the people you love. This kind of betrayal can be as damaging as abandonment itself.

Do you take responsibility for your actions? There comes a time in many relationships when tough conversations need to take place. Sometimes marriages, friendships, or other close relationships are destroyed because neither party is willing to admit they did things to hurt the other person. We always seem to point the finger at the other person. Perhaps you have hurt someone in your life in confronting them with one of their character flaws.

There are times when we need to confront the behavior of another. But before we do, we must first look at our own faults. Jesus asks, "How can you say to your brother, 'Let me take the speck out of your eye, but do not notice the log that is in your own eye?'" (Mt 7:5). Be careful when you confront others that your problem isn't even greater than theirs.

Are you compassionate? Perhaps the greatest thing Jesus taught was to be compassionate to others. Do you show compassion for others? It is one thing to have sympathy and feel sad for those who hurt. It is another to come alongside of them and hold them while they cry.

Compassion is an action much more than an emotion. In the story of the good Samaritan, several people avoided the injured man lying by the side of the road. Perhaps some of these people passing by felt sorry for him. But one man was different. Only he showed a compassionate heart that was moved to action, not merely emotion.

Consider the loved ones in your life today. Do they need your sympathy or a compassion that moves into action? Are you willing to display the love of Christ to those closest to you?

None of us is perfect in the area of interpersonal relationships. If you find yourself falling short in giving yourself to others, perhaps you need to do some habit reforming of your interpersonal skills. Start today by taking on the role of servant to those around you. Bring a wash basin and some towels in case you want to wash a few feet.

MAINTAINING CHRISTIAN INTEGRITY IN OUR PERSONAL LIVES

This area of personal integrity is integrated throughout all aspects of our lives on a daily basis. For the purposes of this chapter, I would like to briefly touch on some of the basic components that contribute to our personal integrity. Specifically, in the next few pages we will look at how well we manage our finances, control the tongue, and display the fruit of the Spirit.

Maintaining financial integrity. Money mismanagement is a bad habit that creeps into the lives of many people. Perhaps you've never had a problem with compulsive spending or have never skimmed money from anyone. But consider the following areas that might signal some financial mismanagement in your life.

The love of money. In the last chapter we touched on the fact that many people are driven by the love of money. Wealth itself does not lead to corruption; it is the love of money that is the root of all evil. However, with a great many people, the more money they accumulate, the more self-sufficient they become. The wealthy must especially guard themselves against greed, arrogance, and pride. Proverbs 28:6 says, "Better is the poor who walks in his integrity, than he who is crooked though he be rich."

Increasing debt. To own a home, especially in some of the major cities where the average cost is well above $200,000, it may be impossible to remain debt-free. But those who are especially bothered by financial mismanagement are those who have allowed the debt in their lives to get out of hand.

One of my rules in using credit cards is that they be paid off in full each month. While there have been times when I needed to pay for a car repair or some other expensive necessity over several months, I try to keep these situations to an absolute minimum.

The best way to keep financial stress from your life is to have absolutely no debt. But the second best option is to keep your debt to an absolute minimum and to always spend within your income.

Limited giving of financial gifts to God. One of our responsibilities as Christians is to give back to God some of the money that he has given to us. In addition to giving to your local church, you may be giving money to organizations that help the poor, or you may be supporting a missionary.

If you consider yourself a committed Christian and are not giving to the Lord's work, perhaps it is time that you make a fresh financial commitment and make every effort to meet it and even exceed it. I once heard a pastor say, "Isn't it amazing how small a twenty-dollar bill looks at the mall but how gigantic it looks in church?"

Compromising personal financial responsibilities. There are so many little ways we tend to compromise our financial integrity. Let's say you found a bag containing $10,000 in cash. The next day you read in the paper that the bag contained the life savings of a little old lady who lived down the street from you. You would probably rush the money to her as quickly as you could. But what if the money was thrown from a car by a drug-dealer under police pursuit? Would you decide that the guy doesn't deserve the money back? Would you withhold it from the police because you think you need the money more than the city does?

Most of us will never face this question, but it's good to consider how much money it would take for you to do something against your Christian principles. I'm reminded of a story about a woman who was approached by a man on the street. The man said, "Excuse me, ma'am, but would you come back to my place with me if I gave you a million dollars?" To which the woman replied, "For a million dollars, I'd do almost anything." So the man continued, "Would you come back to my place for ten dollars?" To which the woman responded, "Of course not. Sir, what do you think I am?" And he replied, "We've already determined that, ma'am. Now we're just trying to decide on the price."

Take caution with regard to your financial integrity as a Christian. If a $200 purchase on your Visa card never showed up, would you report it to the originator? Last year when you did your income tax, did you try to think of ways to fool the IRS? If the woman at the post office accidently gave you two sheets of stamps when you only paid for one, would you let her know? Consider the areas where you compromise financial integrity, then be prepared to clean up your act.

Controlling the tongue. Perhaps the most powerful weapon used in destroying the church is the slippery muscle you find just behind your teeth. Judas used his tongue to betray Jesus. Peter used his to deny him. The crowd used theirs to set Barabbas free instead of the Christ. And still it goes on today. One betrays her friend by breaking the code of confidentiality. Another gossips about the poor job his pastor is doing. And a mother assaults her children with angry words.

The Scriptures are full of instruction to control our tongues. Proverbs 6:16-19 provides seven things that the Lord hates: 1) haughty eyes, 2) a lying tongue, 3) and hands that shed innocent blood, 4) a heart that devises wicked plans, 5) feet that run rapidly to evil, 6) a false witness who utters lies, 7) and one who spreads strife among the brothers.

At least three of these (numbers 2, 6, and 7) have to do with the tongue. God hates it when we lie, when we bear false witness, and when we spread strife among the brothers.

An uncontrollable tongue can be more hurtful than a loaded gun. Consider the following as practices in which you might be participating that not only hurt others but detract from your integrity as a Christian man or woman.

Lying. We are reminded throughout the Word of God to be honest—with God, with others, and with ourselves.

- Keep your tongue from evil and your lips from speaking lies (Ps 34:13).
- Truthful lips endure forever, but a lying tongue lasts only a moment (Prv 12:19).
- A wicked man listens to the evil lips; a liar pays attention to a malicious tongue (Prv 17:4).
- A fortune made by a lying tongue is a fleeting vapor and a deadly snare (Prv 21:6).
- A lying tongue hates those it hurts, and a flattering mouth works ruin (Prv 26:28).

In some cases I believe that God allows us—maybe even honors a lie. Take, for example, those who lied to keep Jews safely in hiding during the holocaust. Or a mother who lies to an intruder to protect the safety of her children. On the other hand, we can use honesty in a hurtful way. If you have strong negative feelings about someone in your life, consider keeping your "honest" feelings to yourself. Speaking your true feelings will only cause them to be hurt and you to be vengeful.

Gossip. Perhaps you can remember a time when someone spread lies or even truths in such a way that it was damaging to others around you or to the spread of the gospel. Few things hurt so deeply. Here are a few Scriptures that reference the harm of gossip.

- A gossip betrays a confidence, but a trustworthy man keeps a secret (Prv 11:13).
- A perverse man stirs up dissension, and a gossip separates close friends (Prv 16:28).
- A gossip betrays a confidence; so avoid a man who talks too much (Prv 20:19).
- Without wood a fire goes out; without gossip a quarrel dies down (Prv 26:20).

Conceit or boastfulness. The Bible has a lot to say about the pride, conceit, and boastfulness we sometimes display. Proverbs 27:1-2 perhaps sums up well this issue: "Do not boast about tomorrow, for you do not know what a day may bring forth. Let another praise you, and not your own mouth; a stranger, and not your own lips."

Vindictiveness. As Christians we are called to speak at all times words that glorify God. Are you guilty of being argumentative, stirring up anger, and speaking words that are venomous? Do you often lose control of your own tongue? Again, Scripture has much to say about this kind of behavior.

- If anyone considers himself religious and yet does not keep a tight rein on his tongue, he deceives himself and his religion is worthless (Jas 1:26).
- Your tongue plots destruction; it is like a sharpened razor, you who practice deceit (Ps 52:2).
- Reckless words pierce like a sword, but the tongue of the wise brings healing (Prv 12:18).

Talking too much. In the last section regarding relationships it was recommended that we listen more than we speak. Not only does listening improve our relationships with others, it shows wisdom.

- When words are many, sin is not absent, but he who holds his tongue is wise (Prv 10:19).
- Even a fool is thought wise if he keeps silent, and discerning if he holds his tongue (Prv 17:28).

Taking the Lord's name in vain. I find foul language offensive, but nothing offends me as much as hearing someone take the name of God or Jesus Christ in vain. The third commandment instructs us to do otherwise: "You shall not misuse the name of the Lord your God, for the Lord will not hold any-one guiltless who misuses his name" (Ex 20:7).

Let your words glorify, affirm, and uplift God's work in your life. Learn to control your tongue.

Displaying the fruit of the Spirit. The purpose of this book is to help us break the bad habits in our spiritual lives so that we may bear more fruit of the Spirit. In this section I want us to focus on some specific ways we can show the characteris-tics listed in Galatians 5:22-23: love, joy, peace, patience, kind-ness, goodness, faithfulness, gentleness, and self-control.

If someone were to describe you as a person, particularly with regard to your walk with God, would these nouns be part of that description? Wouldn't it be nice if people around you said, "He (or she) shows so much love, joy, peace, patience, kindness, goodness, faithfulness, gentleness, and self-control?" In essence Scripture says that these are the very characteristics that separate us from the rest of the world—those who live "of the flesh" (Gal 5:19ff).

In the city where I live there is a Hare Krishna temple. Because of their unusual haircuts and wardrobe, they are quite recognizable around town. In Galatians Paul is telling us that we too should stand out like sore thumbs in the world. Our difference is not like the Hare Krishna dress and haircut; it is in the way we act, in the way we treat others, in the way we deal with adversity, in the way we give to others, in the way we express our love.

Consider the following questions.

Are you able to show love easily? Jesus stated that the greatest commandment is to "love the Lord God with all your heart, and with all your soul, and with all your mind." The second greatest is to "love your neighbor as yourself" (Mt 22:36-39).

- Is your *love for God* obvious to others? Is it obvious to you? In the next chapter we will discuss ways we can grow closer to God through regular time with him.

- Do you express your *love for others* frequently? Don't assume that people close to you are certain that you love them. Love must be communicated verbally, and it must be communicated by the elements discussed a few pages ago with regard to integrity in relationships.

- Do you *love yourself?* Chapter four was dedicated to this very issue of dealing with our self-esteem. God so much wants you to see yourself as the wonderful creation he made you to be. Without this type of love, many of the other fruits of the Spirit are difficult to claim.

How do you handle difficult times? Fruit such as joy, peace, and faithfulness seem to wither and die within many of us when the storms of life threaten us. Divorce. Unemployment. Death of a loved one. Failed friendships. AIDS. Serious accidents. All of these things cause hurt and pain in our lives, but they don't have to affect our joy. Paul reminds us in Ephesians 6 to give thanks in all things. The one who still shows the joy of the Lord, the goodness of her heart, and the faithfulness of a sheep to his shepherd despite the turmoil of life is truly one who is grounded in their relationship with the King of Kings.

Are you able to be frail when you fail? A true sign of a sincere heart is one which is able to show true feelings through natural emotions. I am not saying here that we should let our emotions rule us; one of the fruits of the Spirit, of course, is self-control. On the other hand, far too many people over-control their emotions. Most men, unfortunately, are unable to cry. There is some ridiculous stigma in our society that tears are a sign of weakness.

Jesus himself wept when the storms of life surrounded him. He cried when his friend Lazarus died. He was in so much agony the night he was betrayed that his sweat became as blood. Men and women in the Christian community need to shed their masks of emotional overcontrol to reveal a Christ that cries, says warm things, and yes, even laughs in church.

Do you view others as equal to you? Unfortunately, there is a lot of one-up-manship within the Christian community itself. That's why I've never been much of a denominational animal. One in this denomination thinks her faith is more in line with God's will because her church doesn't believe in infant baptism. Another feels that his cousin isn't really a Christian because he attends a church with too many weekly rituals and not enough freedom of the Spirit. "They're too liberal." "That church only sprinkles. I believe in total immersion." "That denomination ordains women."

But there are disgraces far beyond denominational differences. Many Christians are filled with prejudice and bigotry. A few months ago I visited a museum where there was a special display that explained to children the tragedy of the genocide directed at the Jews by the Nazis during World War II. At the end of the display, children and adults were provided a cardboard tile and some crayons to color a bright picture in the hope that nothing like this would ever happen again. Among the drawings posted was one of a swastika. I removed that particular drawing and threw it in the trash.

I was reminded that the hate that once tragically extinguished so many lives still exists in our world. That experience has stayed with me. My only hope is that some child drew the picture, knowing nothing about its powerful meaning. But I fear there may be people in our churches filled with hate toward Jews, Blacks, Whites, Asians, prisoners, Catholics, Protestants, and any other grouping that is different from them.

Are you bearing fruit? Think about self-control. After reading the chapter prior to this one, have you decided to make some changes to conquer the things that are controlling you? Is the power of God more powerful than the peer pressure in your life?

Think about patience. Are you content with where God has brought you up to this point? Are you able to trust that he will take you the rest of the way?

Think about goodness. A person's goodness is not determined by how much he has. It is determined by how much he gives. Goodness has more to do with being a great servant than it does a great leader.

Think about faithfulness. Are you faithful in your relationship with God, your spouse, your children, and your friends? Do you use the wisdom you've acquired to act wisely? Are you able to accept and walk in God's grace regardless of the situation?

Think about all of these things. But go beyond thinking. To quote a familiar cliché in today's society, "Just do it!" The Spirit of God awaits your fruit-bearing.

MAINTAINING CHRISTIAN INTEGRITY IN THE WORKPLACE

Consider how well you maintain your integrity as a Christian throughout the workweek. Are you the same person sitting at your desk as you are sitting in the pew? Do you treat your co-workers in staff meetings the way you treat fellow parishioners on the patio between services?

While all of the issues we've already discussed regarding integrity within relationships and personal character apply to the workplace also, there are some issues worth discussing that relate specifically to our places of employment. Let's look at the issues we face both in the role of supervisor or employer and in the role of subordinate or employee.

Maintaining Christian integrity as an employer. Depending on the type of employment in which you manage or employ others, maintaining Christian integrity can be especially tough. Perhaps you are a top manager in a highly competitive industry where the profit margin is slim. To maintain company profits you must closely monitor your employees to ensure the most efficient productivity from each. Do you compromise Christian goodness to prod your people toward more efficient work? Maybe your boss is a real bear to work for. Do you relate in a similar way to those who report to you? Let's turn to some more questions to specifically address your role as an employer or supervisor.

Do you put biblical principles above business practices? For companies and organizations to survive, managers have to try their best to see that profits are made or, in the case of nonprofit organizations, that enough money is raised to meet the budget and help more people. Unfortunately, some entities will do almost anything to reach their goals. They step on people, install procedures that border on unethical behavior, and even cross the line into illegal practices. As Christians we are faced with a challenge. We can either confront the things we find dishonest, thereby risking the loss of our job, or we can simply go along with the practices.

Organizations do occasionally need to cut staff members for survival. If you were told today that you had to lay off half of your staff, what would you do differently than, say, a supervisor who is not a Christian? If you own the company, you might offer a severance package beyond what is typical of standard business practices. You might offer to call some others you know in your industry to help your employees find another position. You might contact the employees after they're gone to encourage them.

Try to have your day-to-day conversations, actions, and business practices reflect to all of those around you the love, compassion, and fairness of Christ. And if you show the fruit of the Spirit on Sunday morning, don't appear as a lifeless tree in your role as employer.

Are you a fair employer? The word "fair" is one of those terms like "beauty"—it's often in the eye of the beholder. If you were one of your employees, would you find the policies, work load, and treatment they receive fair? Would you be able to put up with their boss—you? Consider these and the following questions as you begin your next workday.

Do you require too much of your employees? Has the work load in your company or department been evenly distributed? If anyone overworks, try to discover if he stays late because his work load is too great. If you laud him as the most loyal employee, are you being fair to those who work hard but choose to leave at the standard quitting time?

Do you pay them fairly? To verify your answer to this question, you may want to research the amount others in the same field are paying in your part of the country. If you are far below the standards, perhaps you should devise a plan to correct the problem over the next several years. If top executives are paid cash bonuses at the end of the year because of good profits, so should the other employees. During the holidays, are you like Ebenezer Scrooge before or after his dreams?

Do you give them due credit? Many organizations reward their employees for new ideas or suggestions that will save the company money. Do you practice this principle? Do you reward those who have contributed to your success? People are your most valuable asset. They are worth more to you than your "product," your equipment, your bylaws, or your own expertise.

How do you relate with your people? As a supervisor or employer, do you have the heart of Jesus, who came not to be served but to serve? The earlier section regarding Christian integrity in relationships applies here too.

I know a Christian who is feared by all who work for him. Once I asked if he knew that people almost trembled when he was due to arrive at their facility. He replied that he was glad because it keeps the employees on their toes. By contrast, I used to work for the chairman of the board for a large Christian organization. When he entered the room employees seemed to warm up. He had the ability to make people feel like part of a family—even as the organization grew larger.

Could you work for a man or woman like the first one described? Would you, as a top manager, rather have people tremble when you walk into a room or feel a sense of family? Personally, I'd work twice as hard for the latter employer. Consider which of the following options best describe you as a manager or employer.

- When an employee calls in sick, do I make him feel guilty for missing a day of work, or do I inquire if there is anything I can do?
- Do I reprimand employees for suggesting a procedure or policy be changed, or do I carefully consider if their ideas might be better than mine?

- Do I hold back on affirmation for fear the employee will slack off, or do I affirm people with abundance?
- Do I deny my own problems as a manager, or am I willing to change the things about myself that offend employees?
- Do I blame others for my problems and mistakes, or do I take responsibility for my own shortcomings?
- Do I cut employees off mid-sentence or stare at my watch while they're talking, or do I listen to them as I would want to be heard?
- Do I have the attitude that employees are easily replaced, or do I see each as a valuable asset?
- When an employee's production or attitude takes a turn for the worse, do I take action to remove them, or do I find out if there is something I can help them work through?
- Am I short-tempered with difficult employees, or do I display patience?
- Am I a manager who demands to be served or a manager who serves my employees?

Next time you take your employees for granted, look at them through the eyes of Jesus Christ. For he not only died for you but for them.

Maintaining Christian integrity as an employee. Now that we've discussed the role of supervisor, we turn next to a discussion of maintaining Christian integrity as an employee. If you're looking for the perfect employer, he or she doesn't exist. The firm or organization for which you work really has no obligation to be fair, nice, or bearable. If you work for a church, Christian organization, or even a boss who is a fellow believer, you can only hope that they are striving to achieve Christian character as an employer. If Christian integrity is your goal, however, you should strive to be above reproach regardless of how you are being treated.

Do you compromise your Christian principles while at work? Not many people I know could be classified as saints. Our humanness and failures are obvious to all of those closest to us. And they're sometimes most obvious to those with whom we work day by day. Would most people in your workplace be surprised to find that you are a committed Christian?

Few people reading this book blatantly steal money from their employer. But many people in the work force steal from their employers in other, more subtle ways. Consider the following subtle ways an employee can compromise his integrity at work.

- Do you often work less than a full day, arriving at work late and leaving prior to the normal quitting time?
- Have you ever used your employer's stamps or postage meter for your personal mail?
- Do you use the equipment at work (photocopy machine, computer, typewriter, etc.) for personal business without your employer's permission?
- Have you often taken supplies from your office to use at home?
- Do you place non-business expenses such as dinner with your friends or personal mileage on your company expense reports?
- Do you spend more than a few minutes a day making personal telephone calls?
- Do you allow the organization to pay for your personal long-distance phone calls made from work, rather than charging them to your home number?
- If you are hourly and turn in time cards, do you ever include time you did not work?

- Have you ever borrowed from the petty cash fund without reimbursing it?
- Do you justify some of the above actions because you feel you are underpaid or have worked overtime to deserve such "perks"?

Beyond these ways we compromise Christian principles at work, we sometimes do not display the fruit of the Spirit there. Would those around you at work describe you as one displaying goodness, peace, love, faithfulness, and the other qualities of one filled with the Holy Spirit? Or would they find you jealous of the salaries others are earning, angry at your co-workers, and causing regular disputes?

How do you relate with your employer or supervisor? John 13:16 says that "a slave is not greater than his master." All of us need to show proper respect for those who supervise us. Almost anyone can show goodness when surrounded by the same. The true test of Christian character is showing goodness amid adversity, unfairness, and unkindness.

One of the biggest challenges for any of us to face is the ability to reflect the fruit of the Spirit when we work for a difficult person. If, however, an employer is too much for you to bear and is causing you emotional strife, perhaps you should serve him to the best of your ability and actively seek another position.

If you work for a good person or organization, count your blessings. Consider giving your supervisor words of encouragement or cards showing your appreciation. Affirmation does not always come from the top down; it needs to flow the other way too.

Consider the following questions with regard to how well you relate with your employer, whether or not he or she fits either of the above descriptions.

- Are you able to accept and learn from criticism and recommendations for performance improvement?
- Do you show as much compassion for your supervisor when things get rough in her life as you would want her to show you?
- Have you tried to improve your employer/employee relationship?
- Do you work just as hard for your organization when the boss is away as you do when he or she is present?

Whatever you do in your workplace, make it pleasing to the Lord rather than to men.

MAINTAINING INTEGRITY IN CHRISTIAN ORGANIZATIONS

Before we leave this topic of maintaining Christian integrity beyond Sunday morning, we should address issues regarding those who work either in the church or for a Christian organization and those who are active as lay people in the leadership of these organizations. Unfortunately, Christian organizations are not immune to any of the habits discussed in this chapter or elsewhere in the book.

I have worked with dozens of churches and Christian non-profit organizations around the country. At one time I worked with fifty rescue missions, helping them raise funds in order to feed, shelter, and share the gospel with as many homeless people as possible. I loved working with rescue missions and spent more than a third of the year visiting them throughout the United States. A typical five-day week would take me to five different cities.

The first time I visited one particular city I was in for a surprise. Instead of stepping from the jetway and walking to a taxi as was my routine, the mission director and his wife met me at the plane. When we got to the car, they had a nicely wrapped gift waiting for me. Instead of the typical hotel, they made arrangements for me to stay in a cozy bed-and-break-fast place. Then they took me on a tour of the area. These were two of the most caring, loving, giving, and compassion-ate people I've known. The fruit of the Spirit was obvious in their lives.

At a meeting with the board of directors for this particular mission, the director and his wife were asked to leave the room so that the board could discuss their salary review. I was shocked to find out the near-poverty-level salaries of this cou-ple. Knowing that the director and his wife didn't use their heater in the freezing cold winters because they couldn't afford the utility bills, I hoped that they would receive a huge raise to bring their salaries to a more reasonable level. Unfor-tunately my hopes were in vain.

I managed to maintain control and stay quiet. After all, I wasn't there to comment on any part of their agenda other than fundraising. I knew that the directors would go on giv-ing gifts and meeting people at the airport, never complain-ing about their salaries. They weren't in it for the money. The board left for their warm homes in their nice cars that cold evening. I wonder how many of them knew what it's like to raise a family with several children on the salary these people were making.

I don't believe that anyone should enter the ministry for financial gain. Some in ministry positions are probably paid too much money. On the other hand, if you are involved in the leadership of any church or Christian organization, look carefully at what you are paying employees. Could you sur-vive on what these people are making? When your pastor goes to the market for food or to the mall for clothing, does he or she get a forty percent discount simply because his income is forty percent less than the rest of society? Of course not. Many people object, and rightfully so, when leaders of nonprofit organizations misuse money or are significantly overpaid. Few speak up when they see the poor salaries earned by many loving, devoted Christian workers.

Pastors and leaders of Christian organizations should especially be aware of the bad habits discussed throughout this chapter. Your role as leader should not be misinterpreted as a license to control others. Like Jesus, our role is to serve—not only our congregations and needy people, but those with whom we work most closely. Are the fruits of the Spirit obvious in your board or elder meetings? Are you displaying goodness, love, peace, and faithfulness in your words and actions?

AN INTEGRITY ANALYSIS

Unlike the ants mentioned earlier who scurry along destroying everything in their path, Christians are called to work together as a powerful force for good, displaying the fruit of the Spirit to all the world. Whether at work, at home, or at the supermarket, we need to maintian our Christian character in the little things we do each day. Perhaps some issues presented in this chapter challenged you to seek change. Let's look now at a few steps that can help you turn from your bad habits and develop good ones.

Step One: Evaluate your Christian character. Before we can begin to change some of the bad habits discussed in this chapter, we must first pinpoint the areas where we most need to focus. Check the response (A or B) that best completes the following sentences.

In my close family relationships and friendships, I...

1. ____ A. spend regular quality time with them weekly.
   ____ B. have been too busy lately to see much of them.

2. ____ A. almost always keep my commitments with them.
   ____ B. am often canceling my time with them.

3. ____ A. keep promises made to them.
   ____ B. have broken many promises lately.

4. ____ A. honor their confidentiality when they share something is private.
   ____ B. don't keep secrets very well.

5. ____ A. focus much of my time on serving them.
   ____ B. spend too much of my time on my own needs.

6. ____ A. listen more than I talk.
   ____ B. talk more than I listen.

7. ____ A. usually accept their idiosyncracies.
   ____ B. am always telling them how they should change.

8. ____ A. take time to hear their perspective on things.
   ____ B. usually don't try to understand their perspective.

9. ____ A. verbally affirm them quite often.
   ____ B. criticize them more than I affirm them.

10. ____ A. physically affirm them with hugs or other signs.
    ____ B. am afraid to show any physical affirmation.

11. ____ A. say "I love you" often.
    ____ B. rarely express my love for them.

12. ____ A. am very loyal.
    ____ B. have not been very loyal lately.

13. ____ A. always speak highly of them to others.
    ____ B. often say negative things about them to others.

14. ____ A. take responsibility when I've hurt them.
    ____ B. often blame them for hurting me.

15. ____ A. show active compassion when they hurt.
    ____ B. feel sad when they hurt but rarely am able to comfort them.

16. ____ A. try to model Christ's love in my relationship with them.
    ____ B. probably do not reflect Christ's love to them most of the time.

The following best describes my personal character, whether at home, at church, or when alone.

17. ____ A. I spend well within my income.
    ____ B. I spend beyond my financial means.

18. ____ A. I love money.
    ____ B. Money is not essential for my joy.

19. ____ A. I do not have a great deal of debt.
    ____ B. I am in debt over my head.

20. ____ A. I give regularly to God's ministries.
    ____ B. I seldom give to God's ministries.

21. ____ A. I often give beyond my regular gifts.
    ____ B. I seldom give beyond my regular giving.

22. ____ A. I do not lie.
    ____ B. I've told several lies lately.

23. ____ A. I seldom gossip about others.
    ____ B. I gossip about others fairly regularly.

24. ____ A. I never talk with conceit.
    ____ B. I praise myself to others quite often.

25. _____ A. I keep a tight reign on my tongue.
    _____ B. I am often argumentative or deceitful with my words.

26. _____ A. I am not verbose.
    _____ B. I talk way too much.

27. _____ A. My words are not offensive to God.
    _____ B. I take the Lord's name in vain.

28. _____ A. I display the fruit of the Spirit more than I do the works of the flesh.
    _____ B. I display the works of the flesh more than I do the fruit of the Spirit.

29. _____ A. My love for God is obvious to others.
    _____ B. Others are probably not aware of my love for God.

30. _____ A. Joy remains in my life even when things get tough.
    _____ B. The joy in my life dissipates when things get tough.

31. _____ A. I usually reveal honest, real emotions.
    _____ B. I have trouble revealing my true emotions.

32. _____ A. I view all others as equal to me.
    _____ B. I consider myself better than some others.

33. _____ A. I am not prejudiced toward other religions, races, or classes of people.
    _____ B. I consider some groups of people inferior to others.

As a supervisor or employer I...

34. _____ A. put biblical principles before business practices.
    _____ B. focus more on business than I do on goodness.

35. _____ A. treat my employees as I would like to be treated.
    _____ B. would have problems working for a boss like me.

36. ____ A. often put myself in my employees' shoes.
    ____ B. seldom place myself in the shoes of my employees.

37. ____ A. pay employees fairly.
    ____ B. pay employees below the industry standard.

38. ____ A. always give credit where credit is due.
    ____ B. am benefiting from my employees' work without giving them due credit.

39. ____ A. see and treat employees as my most valuable asset.
    ____ B. feel that people can be easily replaced.

40. ____ A. serve more than I expect to be served.
    ____ B. rarely have an attitude of servanthood toward employees.

41. ____ A. feel that employees see me as a kind person.
    ____ B. feel I must be tough to keep employees on their toes.

42. ____ A. affirm employees regularly.
    ____ B. seldom affirm people I supervise.

43. ____ A. listen carefully when employees are speaking.
    ____ B. cut employees off when I feel they are wasting my time.

44. ____ A. ask employees if I can help when they seem upset.
    ____ B. have little patience with people whose work is affected by personal problems.

As an employee I...

45. ____ A. usually maintain my character as a Christian.
    ____ B. think co-workers might be surprised to find that I'm a Christian.

46. ____ A. work full days except on rare occasions.
    ____ B. often arrive late, leave early, or call in sick when I'm well.

47. ____ A. never use my employer's property for personal use unless I have specific permission.
    ____ B. use the organization's postage and equipment for personal use without specific permission.

48. ____ A. do not think of myself as being better than my supervisor.
    ____ B. think of myself as being greater than my supervisor.

49. ____ A. show the fruit of the Spirit even when situations at work get difficult.
    ____ B. display works of the flesh when things don't go well.

50. ____ A. affirm my supervisor as often as possible.
    ____ B. would never affirm the person I work for.

51. ____ A. am able to accept criticism or suggestions for improving my performance.
    ____ B. usually deny that I need to change when recommendations are made.

52. ____ A. work just as hard when my boss is gone as when he or she is away.
    ____ B. take advantage of times when my boss is away.

In my role as pastor, church staff member, Christian organization worker, or ministry lay leader I...

53. ____ A. display goodness, patience, and love in my relationships with all others involved in the ministry.
    ____ B. have been known to treat people in the ministry unkindly, often displaying works of the flesh.

54. ____ A. make a point not to gossip about others in the ministry.

____ B. gossip quite often about others involved in the ministry.

55. ____ A. do my part to make sure others in the ministry are paid and treated with integrity.

____ B. feel people in ministry should live on less than average salaries.

56. ____ A. try to display Christ's love to others around me.

____ B. may have turned some people away from Christ because of my works of the flesh in relating with them.

57. ____ A. use my authority in Christian leadership appropriately, demonstrating servant leadership and compassion.

____ B. have used my authority in Christian leadership inappropriately through misuse of power and hurtful words.

58. ____ A. am committed to compassionately help resolve issues when I see people being mistreated within the ministry.

____ B. turn my head and hope that problems in the ministry will go away.

59. ____ A. affirm my fellow pastors, staff members, elders, board members, and others around me as often as I can.

____ B. seldom affirm others in the ministry with me.

60. ____ A. have forgiven others who have hurt me in this or previous ministry situations.

____ B. am still hurt or bitter regarding this or some past ministry situation.

Step Two: Develop objectives for change. Look at the items above for which you checked the "B" choice. Then, in the space below or on a separate piece of paper, create objectives by writing the "A" statements that correspond to these same items. If you wish to paraphrase the objective so that it more directly applies to your situation, please do so.

Most of us will probably have a list longer than two or three items. If your list of objectives is long, use the column at the right to rank them 1 through 15, listing the characteristics you think most important to change first. If you're brave, you might ask someone close to you to assist in ranking the issues that most need attention. Here is an example to help you develop your own objectives list.

Darcy's Objectives for Improving Her Christian Character

Number from list	Objective	Rank
6.	Try my best to talk less and really listen to those I love.	2
20.	Begin this Sunday to give a regular weekly gift to the church.	4
31.	Seek help to overcome my fears of displaying real emotions.	3
46.	Arrive at work on time beginning tomorrow.	5
60.	Meet with Marge from the trustee board to help heal our hurt.	1

Objectives for Improving My Own Christian Character

Number from list	Objective	Rank
_____	_____	_____
	_____	

Number from list	Objective	Rank
___	_____	___
	_____	
___	_____	___
	_____	
___	_____	___
	_____	
___	_____	___
	_____	
___	_____	___
	_____	
___	_____	___
	_____	
___	_____	___
	_____	
___	_____	___
	_____	
___	_____	___
	_____	
___	_____	___
	_____	
___	_____	___
	_____	
___	_____	___
	_____	

Now, so that you are not too overwhelmed or discouraged with the number of things you'd like to work on, focus on just the first three as you move on to Step Three.

Step Three: Seek change. On several sheets of paper or three-by-five cards, list today's date. Then write your top three objectives on each. Place a copy wherever you spend private time daily, for example, taped to your bathroom mirror, attached to the visor in your car, inside your Bible, on your desk at work.

Each time you look at a card, read all three items to see if you've made any progress. Once you feel you've made great strides in changing your habit for the better, replace the improved habit with the next one in priority.

Darcy's first set of cards would look like this:

June 12, 1992

1. Meet with Marge from the trustee board to help heal our hurt.
2. Try my best to talk less and really listen to those I love.
3. Seek help to overcome my fears of displaying real emotions.

If Darcy meets with Marge for lunch on June 20 and her issues are appropriately resolved, she can cross that item off her card, leave the other two, and add the item she ranked fourth.

The goal is to check your card every week or two to see how you are doing on changing the habits you seek to change. Try to add new, fresh challenges regularly. Use your time practicing the spiritual disciplines outlined in the next chapter in seeking these changes. Pray that your character as a Christian can grow with each day. Find Scriptures to study that relate to your particular issues. Ask your support group to help you focus on the areas where you want to improve.

Step Four: Regular review of your progress. As you seek to change those daily habits that prevent the fruits of the Spirit from bearing their best harvest, reevaluate yourself regularly. Mark your calendar to reanalyze the habits mentioned in this chapter ninety days from now. Then set a time ninety days after that. Along with your objective cards, post the following chart in the same familiar areas that you frequent daily.

Today...

have I practiced the works of the flesh?	*or displayed the fruit of the Spirit?*
immorality	love
impurity	joy
sensuality	peace
idolatry	patience
sorcery	kindness
enmity	goodness
strife	faithfulness
jealousy	gentleness
outbursts of anger	self-control
disputes	
dissension	
factions	
envy	
drunkenness	
carousing	

If we live by the Spirit, let us also walk by the Spirit. **Gal 5:19-26**

SEVEN

I'll Start Tomorrow... If I Have the Time

* * *

Practicing Spiritual Disciplines in a Busy World

Remain in me, and I will remain in you. No branch can bear fruit by itself; it must remain in the vine. Neither can you bear fruit unless you remain in me.

Jn 15:3

Habits that Hurt

Staying too busy to include God
Avoiding spiritual disciplines
Lacking a weekly Sabbath

Symptoms

Limited Bible study
Infrequent prayer
Sporadic worship
Fear of solitude
Lack of community involvement

Habits that Heal

Spending private time with God daily
Attending regular weekly worship
Participating in community

* * *

WHERE HAVE WE COME THUS FAR IN THE BOOK? In the first two chapters we discussed the topics of maintaining a faith that can survive the cloudy days and accepting the incredible free gift of grace from God. In dealing with these two topics we came face-to-face with some of the basics of our Christian walk and the way we relate to God the Father. We moved next into two chapters that dealt with forgiveness— how to forgive others and how to forgive ourselves. In the following two chapters we talked about the habits we face from outside influences and the way we display our internal character.

All of these topics interrelate. In dealing with dependencies we must learn to forgive ourselves and others. In learning to accept the grace of God, we must face the fact of our imperfections and realize that our character will not always be what we'd like it to be. We sometimes allow our trust in God to waver when our self-esteem is low.

All of the topics discussed thus far have been offered as common issues that Christians struggle with. An interesting transition seems to take place as we grow in our faith. Once we realize that God loves us, through his grace, regardless of how well or poorly we measure up, we begin to seek change because of who he is. We begin to desire a life pleasing to him.

If humanity never knew that a loving, compassionate God existed, there would be little reason to change. We'd move aimlessly through life, driven only by our own fleshly desires and needs for satisfaction. Thankfully, God has shown himself to us, and we desire to be like him.

But we can't do it alone. We can make commitments that will strengthen our willpower and self-control. Friends can encourage and support us as we seek change. But there is really only one way we can have a heart that truly reaches for God. If you seek change in your life, nothing is more important in your plan to change than are the elements described in this chapter—those which help us spend private and community time with the Lord Jesus Christ.

ENCOUNTERING CHRIST

Have you ever noticed yourself picking up habits from your spouse, close friends, or those with whom you work? Perhaps you've begun to speak some of their phrases, to laugh like them, to practice their habits. As part of the seminar I teach for Prison Fellowship Ministries, we encourage inmates who are about to be released to make decisions regarding who they will spend time with. If they return to the people they used to spend time with and those people still participate in the kinds of activities that led them to jail, the inmate's chances of returning to prison are unfortunately much stronger. If on the other hand, they settle in with a new group of friends, perhaps by becoming active in a local church or fellowship, new patterns can be learned.

In much the same way, those of us who want to grow in Christ can only do so by developing a closer relationship with him. It's unlikely that any bad habits can be eliminated nor any good habits be implemented without a commitment to regular participation in the spiritual disciplines such as those discussed in this chapter. There are no shortcuts for spiritual growth, yet spiritual growth does not have to be difficult. Through regular, daily communication with God, we move closer to him. He can lead us out of the darkest tunnel and lift us from the deepest abyss. He is with us always, though we're not always with him.

Many Christians wonder why their faith is so out of focus, yet they spend less than a few minutes each week focusing on God. In John 15:4 Jesus says that "no branch can bear fruit unless you remain in the vine. Neither can you bear fruit unless you remain in me." This is just one Scripture that emphasizes the importance of spiritual disciplines. Our daily walk with Jesus is essential to our continued spiritual nourishment.

We encounter Christ through the Scriptures given to us, through the proclamation of his word, and through the sacraments. All three are important to our developing new habits that heal. In this chapter we will look at a few of the basic spiritual disciplines important to growing close to Christ and to maintaining spiritual growth. There are a number of good books on the market that describe at length these and many other spiritual disciplines discussed throughout the Bible.

SOLITUDE AND COMMUNITY: A BALANCE

How do we participate in the spiritual disciplines that keep us close to God? It is important that we balance our time with him. Part of our relationship with the Lord Jesus Christ is private and requires that we spend time alone with God. But another important part of our growth comes when we actively participate in a community with other believers.

There are many people who spend hours privately reading the Scriptures and praying to God. Other people spend a great deal of time in their church activities but seem to almost fear times alone with God. Both types of people can be sincerely committed Christians. Each has good habits of spiritual discipline. But each has some imbalance with regard to their focus on community and solitude. Perhaps Dietrich Bonhoeffer, my favorite Christian author, stated best the pitfalls of having solitude without community and vice versa:

One who wants fellowship without solitude plunges into the void of words and feelings, and one who seeks solitude without fellowship perishes in the abyss of vanity, self-infatuation and despair. Let him who cannot be alone beware of community. Let him who is not in community beware of being alone.[1]

The need for community. While eighty percent of people describe themselves as Protestant or Catholic, only forty percent say they attend church regularly. Recently I read an article in the paper on the reasons people don't attend church. I've paraphrased some of them below:

- Weekends are my only time away from work. Church services take too much of my free time.
- Churches are always asking for money. My budget is already too tight.
- The church believes that the only people who go to heaven are those who accept Jesus Christ as their personal Savior. If that's the truth, I don't want any part of him or the church.
- I worship God in my own way, and frankly, I feel it's more honorable than the way most churches honor him.
- All I find there are hypocrites. If I want to find those, I'll simply go to work or turn on the television.
- After my strict upbringing in Catholic schools, I never want to return to any kind of organized religion.
- I disagree with the church politically regarding abortion and other social concerns.
- The church preaches too much Hell and damnation. If God is so good, why does he want us to constantly be reminded that we might burn in Hell?

Despite what the surveys show as to why people don't attend church, community is important in the continuing life of Christian people. Without the support of fellow believers, many Christians shrivel up and die spiritually.

The early church had a commitment to the community of fellow believers. Acts 2:42 and following says, "And they were continually devoting themselves to the apostles' teaching and to fellowship, to the breaking of bread and to prayer." We are called today as were the early believers to hold one another up during times of trial and adversity. While we must keep our individual walk with God on course, community is equally as essential.

I love to stroll along the tide pools down at the beach. One particular point where I walk reaches out almost a hundred yards from the shore when the tide is low. Clinging to the rocks that make up this point are thousands of mussel shells. The shells that individually cling to the rocks are fragile and easily broken if stepped on. When they are grouped together in large numbers, however, I've noticed that you can easily walk upon these shells without causing any damage to them. Alone they are broken; close together they support one another.

The need for solitude. Some solitude in our walk with Christ is quite healthy. Jesus himself went to a "lonely place" many times throughout his ministry on earth. Quite often the Greek word used to describe his time alone literally meant "wilderness" or "desert." Here are some Scriptures describing Jesus' own times of solitude:

1. After Jesus' baptism, Matthew 4:1 says, "Jesus was led up by the Spirit into the wilderness to be tempted by the devil."
2. Following the death of John the Baptist, we read in Matthew 14:13, "Now when Jesus heard it, he withdrew from there in a boat, to a lonely place by himself."
3. One night Jesus healed many who were ill and cast out many demons. In Mark 1:35 we find the words, "And in the early morning, while it was still dark, he arose and went out and departed to a lonely place, and was praying there."

4. Before he chose his disciples, Luke 6:12 says, "And it was at this time that he went off to the mountain to pray, and he spent the whole night in prayer to God."

5. After feeding the five thousand, Matthew 14:23 reads, "And after he had sent the multitudes away, he went up to the mountain by himself to pray; and when it was evening he was there alone."

6. And just before he was to be betrayed, Matthew 26:36 says, "Then Jesus came with them to a place called Gethsemane, and said to his disciples, 'Sit here while I go over there and pray.'"

In just these few examples we can see how often Jesus spent time in solitude. Let's look at the various settings in these Scriptures to learn from Jesus when withdrawing to a time of solitude and prayer is appropriate.

No. Event in Jesus' life (above)	Application to our lives
1. After His baptism	Following blessed events
1. Prior to being tempted by the devil	Before temptation comes near
2. After the death of John the Baptist	During times of grief or despair
3. After Jesus heals many	After helping someone in need
3. During the early morning	Before we begin our day
4. Before selecting his disciples	Prior to a big decision
4. Throughout the night	During the night
5. After feeding the five thousand	After witnessing a miracle
5. When it was evening	At the close of the day
6. Just before his betrayal	When others hurt us

Of course, this list is not exhaustive. Yet even with these few verses, we can see that Jesus retreated into solitude during all parts of the day and before or after major events, whether they were blessed or difficult. Time alone with his Father was important to Jesus.

Certain kinds of solitude can be quite harmful. Our time of solitude should not be based on a vindictive retreat from fellow believers. Rather, it should be a personal time, completely away from others both physically and mentally, in order that we can be in the presence of God.

There are a great many people who fear being alone. Perhaps these people confuse the principle of solitude with that of being lonely. The latter term is affiliated with feelings of detachment, isolation, seclusion, or rejection. Solitude is quite the opposite. Although it represents a time away from people and the noise of our busy world, it does not indicate isolation. For solitude is a time of joining together with God. Once you accept Christ in your life, you can never be truly alone.

THE DISCIPLINES: WHAT, WHY, AND HOW?

As previously mentioned, other authors have written eloquently about a wide range of spiritual disciplines for us to follow. They include regular prayer, an ongoing devotional life, worship, Bible study and reflection, and service to others—the areas upon which I'd like to focus in this chapter. All of these disciplines are important in our time with community and in our times of solitude. Prayer allows us to communicate with God. Consistent devotions help us to be more knowledgeable about God. And service gives us an opportunity to display God to others.

In Matthew 6 Jesus provides a very important requirement for our participation in spiritual disciplines: that we participate humbly and without public announcement. With regard to stewardship he says, "When therefore you give alms, do not sound a trumpet before you, as the hypocrites do in the synagogues and in the streets" (Mt 6:2-4). With regard to prayer he says, "And when you pray, you are not to be as the hypocrites; for they love to stand and pray in the synagogues and on the street corners, in order to be seen by men" (Mt 6:5-7). And in addressing fasting he says, "And whenever you fast, do not put on a gloomy face as the hypocrites do, for they neglect their appearance in order to be seen fasting by men" (Mt 6:16-18).

Let's turn now to a discussion of the spiritual disciplines that are the focus of this chapter.

Prayer. Volumes have been written about prayer, so the next few pages will only scratch the surface of this topic. Prayer provides our link of communication with God. But it is a spiritual discipline that seems to intimidate a great many believers, especially those who are new in Christ. For those who have been Christians for many years, prayer usually seems to come more naturally.

I, too, can remember the fear inside years ago when someone asked me to pray aloud in a group. Perhaps many feel this fear because they are afraid to fail before God, as if a few flubbed words in a prayer would hurt him in some way. I once heard someone say that prayer should be just as easy as talking with our father or closest friend. In every sense of the word, it is exactly that!

People struggle not only with the content of their prayers; they also wonder about its effectiveness. If we pray without believing that prayer is effective, we need to journey further in our walk with God. It is for this reason that I included the topic of prayer in the final chapter. For if we don't trust that God is real, aren't able to see his gift of grace as miraculous, and don't need him to change the parts in our lives that hurt, it may not make much sense to pray.

Fortunately, God does hear all of our prayers. Remember how he heard your first unsophisticated prayer when you asked him into your life? Think about what he's done in your life since then. It just may help your belief in the power of prayer.

Also, when we pray, we must keep in mind the will of God. If he answered all of our prayers with an affirmative response, he wouldn't be God—we would. Sometimes God's answer is "no." And sometimes he asks us to be patient and wait many years for his reply.

One of the reasons prayer intimidates new and mature Christians alike is the fact that so many don't understand how to pray. They're afraid that perhaps they might leave something out, say the wrong words, include something inappropriate as part of their prayer, or offend God somehow. One of the great things about prayer is that our prayer life is just as unique as our own personal relationship with God the Father.

Some people have a special gift of knowing what to pray and how to pray for it. I remember the gift of prayer that one of my seminary professors had. The first day of class, he was somehow able to know exactly how I was feeling inside. His prayer was insightful, comforting, and pertinent to whatever I was feeling. To be honest, I don't remember exactly what he prayed for. But I do remember how I felt during his prayer.

Let's look at six elements you might want to consider including in your private and community prayer life. Not every element is required in each prayer.

Praise. Our prayers should include a time of praising God for being the Creator and Savior of the world. In beginning our prayers with this element, we come to him in humility, honoring and revering his glorious name. I suggest you read through the Psalms and find some that offer words of praise that are particularly meaningful to you. Think of the wonder of God's world—the vastness of the seas, the beauty of creation, and the infinite expanse of the universe.

Thanksgiving. On the fourth Thursday of November each year, families gather around their dinner tables to thank God for all they have. While this is a holiday of great warmth for Americans, our hearts should be filled with thanksgiving throughout the year. Following your time of praise and reverence, thank God for all that he has provided: your faith, your family, your friends, your health, your talents, his Son. Every day, no matter how difficult life gets, we can find several things for which to thank God.

Confession. Perhaps you have heard or seen illustrations that describe sin as a barrier or a deep chasm that separates us from God. 1 John 1:9 says, "If we confess our sins, he is faithful and righteous to forgive us our sins and to cleanse us from all unrighteousness." Confession near the beginning of a prayer destroys any boundaries and fills in the deepest of chasms, allowing us to open up our communication with God. Pray for the sins of which you are aware, and pray for those of which you are not.

Intercession. Throughout his letters Paul asks fellow Christians to pray for him. Paul himself prayed consistently for the people in the churches he visited, both when he was with them and when he was away. We too are to pray for the others in our lives: the sick, the unsaved, those whom we're close to, those in leadership.

Petition. Philippians 4:6 offers the basis for this element, where we offer to God prayers for our own needs. It says, "Be anxious for nothing, but in everything by prayer and supplication with thanksgiving let your requests be made known to God." This is the time in our prayer when we come before the Lord in our humility—telling him our hurts, asking him for help.

Listening. Too often we consider our prayer time to be a speech offered to God. Some of the most effective prayer time is that which is silent, waiting and listening to the Word of God.

The Lord provided a prayer for us to follow. When something is troubling me enough that I awaken in the middle of the night, I often go through the Lord's Prayer and apply its elements to my own needs. Consider the following example of how someone might follow the Lord's Prayer in their personal prayer time.

Line from the Lord's Prayer	Personal Application
Our Father, who art in heaven	My Father, who reigns over everything
Hallowed be thy name	You are the most Holy One
Thy kingdom come	You are at the center of my heart

Thy will be done
    on earth as it is in heaven
	Only you know your will for
	    my life

Give us this day our daily bread	You promise to provide for me

And forgive us our debts,
    as we also have forgiven our
    debtors
	Help me to forgive…
	    as you have forgiven me
	    for…

And lead us not into temptation,
    but deliver us from evil
	Free me, Lord, from the
	    temptation of…

For thine is the kingdom,
    and the power, and the glory
    forever.
	All these things are possible
	    only because of you.

When you recite the Lord's Prayer from memory, do more than merely let the words roll off the end of your tongue without meaning. Apply them to your own life.

DEVOTIONAL LIFE

The second spiritual discipline upon which we will focus is that of maintaining a regular devotional life. Jesus quoted from Deuteronomy when he confronted the devil: "Man shall not live by bread alone, but on every word that proceeds out of the mouth of God." God provided manna as physical nourishment for the nation of Israel during its forty years in the wilderness. But his promises and words provided so much more—spiritual nourishment to survive the good and tough times. And so it is with us today. Just as we cannot survive physically without food, we cannot survive spiritually without the Word of God. If you are not involved in the habit of participating in regular community *and* private devotional life, consider adding the following activities to your schedule.

Community devotions. We've briefly mentioned the early church, who were "day by day continuing with one mind in the temple, and breaking bread from house to house, they were taking their meals together with gladness and sincerity of heart, praising God, and having favor with all the people. And the Lord was adding to their number day by day those who were being saved" (Acts 2:46-47). Hebrews 10:24-25 encourages community with one another: "Let us consider how to stimulate one another to love and good deeds, not forsaking our own assembling together, as is the habit of some, but encouraging one another, and all the more, as you see the day drawing near."

The Lord God did not intend for us to worship him entirely in private. He calls us to eat together, stimulate one another to good deeds, encourage one another, and spread together the gospel of Jesus Christ. If you choose to remain private with all of your worship and study, you are missing out on one of the blessings of Christian life.

Studying the Scriptures. Unfortunately, there are a great many active Christians who haven't picked up their Bible in months—maybe years. Oh, they attend church on Sunday and listen intently to the pastor's sermon. Yet they think Jonah is either the name of a whale or the name of Noah's boat. I am not picking on the new Christian who is still trying to understand how to find her way around the Scriptures. I *am* addressing the person who has known Christ for many years but who knows very little about his teachings.

We are lucky today in that there is a vast amount of material written and designed for people to read the Bible in one year. But staying on course requires personal discipline.

If you have trouble disciplining yourself to study the Scriptures on your own, I recommend participation in an organized Bible study through your church or through national organizations such as Bible Study Fellowship. This organization provides a format that integrates three different settings for Bible study. First, each person prepares his own lesson *individually*. The lesson plans provide Scripture assignments and questions that support ideal guidelines for private daily devotions. Second, the lesson plans are discussed *in a small group setting* so one can learn from the experiences of other believers. Third, the Scriptures are taught *by a knowledgeable instructor*. I recommend all three types of regular Bible study—individual, small group, and educational—for a balanced devotional life.

Journaling. One of the best tools I know for maintaining daily communication with God is the use of a journal. For eight years I have made daily entries in my simple journal, which consists of lined paper in a three-ringed notebook. Some journals take on the form of a diary where the writer's spiritual life is chronicled. Others consist of prayer requests or lists of praises and thanksgiving. Often a journal records significant Scriptures and personal responses to the same.

The use of a journal guarantees that I spend some time with God every day—even if it is only for a few minutes. It can be the key to maintaining a consistent devotional life and regular communication with the Father.

Honor the Lord's Day. The fourth commandment instructs us to "remember the Sabbath day, to keep it holy." Just as God rested on the seventh day from his works of creation, we too are to take a day away from our labors.

Jesus was more concerned that we understand the purpose of the Sabbath than he was in encouraging a ritualistic or legalistic approach to the fourth commandment. While time off from our work is important physically and emotionally, the Sabbath provides a time for us to rest from the preoccupation with working, succeeding, reaching financial goals and the like. It is a time to remind ourselves that our reason for living is to worship God, not to toil for some worldly goals.

SERVICE TO OTHERS

From the beginning of Matthew 24 through the first two verses of chapter 26, Jesus is describing to his disciples his return to earth in the end times. In Matthew 25:31-46 he is talking specifically about the judgment that will come at that time.

"But when the Son of Man comes in his glory, and all the angels with him, then he will sit on his glorious throne. And all the nations will be gathered before him; and He will separate them from one another, as the shepherd separates the sheep from the goats; and he will put the sheep on his right, and the goats on his left.

"Then the King will say to those on his right, 'Come, you who are blessed of my Father, inherit the kingdom prepared for you from the foundation of the world. For I was hungry, and you gave me something to eat; I was thirsty, and you gave me drink; I was a stranger, and you invited me in; naked and you clothed me; I was sick and you visited me; I was in prison, and you came to me.'

"Then the righteous will answer him saying, 'Lord, when did we see you hungry, and feed you, or thirsty, and give you drink? And when did we see you a stranger, and invite you in, or naked, and clothe you? And when did we see you sick, or in prison, and come to you?'

"And the King will answer and say to them, 'Truly I say to you, to the extent that you did it to one of these brothers of mine, even to the least of them, you did it to me.'

"Then he will also say to those on his left, 'Depart from me, accursed ones, into the eternal fire which has been prepared for the devil and his angels; for I was hungry, and you gave me nothing to eat; I was thirsty, and you gave me nothing to drink; I was a stranger, and you did not invite me in; naked and you did not clothe me; sick, and in prison, and you did not visit me.'

"Then they themselves will answer, saying, 'Lord, when did we see you hungry, or thirsty, or a stranger, or naked, or sick, or in prison, and did not take care of you?' Then he will answer them, saying, 'Truly I say to you, to the extent that you did not do it to one of the least of these, you did not do it to me.' And these will go away into eternal punishment, but the righteous into eternal life."

I know a young man named Trevor who for nine years was addicted to drugs and alcohol. His life and that of his family were marked by pain, fear, violence, guilt, and despair. There were emergency rooms, wrecked cars, jails, and courtrooms. Finally his family had to expel him from their home. Trevor became a street person, living in old cars, vacant houses, and junk yards.

Somehow Trevor's basic honor, decency, and honesty would not leave him. Even during the bad years he saved a friend's life and was usually the first to go to another's aid.

Today Trevor is a hard worker who studies in his spare time. He has a special compassion for street people. "Sometimes," he says, "I stop the car and offer to take them wherever they need to go; other times I empty my pockets for them, hoping they will get a warm meal."

When Trevor was at the depth of his despair, living on the streets, he probably fit very well into the category of "the least of these" found in the above Scripture. He often went hungry, certainly was sick with addiction, and probably felt deep loneliness. When Trevor returned as a respected member of society, he didn't forget about his times among the least of these.

Do we have to live on the streets to have a heart for the homeless? Must we spend a week in prison to feel the loneliness of inmates locked behind cold steel bars? Jesus' words above are not directed only to those who have felt like the least of these at some time during their lives. Service to others is one of the spiritual disciplines Jesus addresses throughout the Scriptures. Here are several suggestions of how you might become more involved in service to others.

Serving those in your home or family. Sometimes the people who need our help most are those we see every day. Perhaps there is someone close to you who is going through a difficult time right now and would simply enjoy your company. You might know of a project that someone needs done. Maybe your children need you to spend more time with them. There are lots of suggestions of how to spend time with those you love in my books, *52 Simple Ways to Say "I Love You"* and *52 Simple Ways to Have Fun with Your Child*. Consider using some of these ideas, or make up some of your own.

Serving those in your church. Often churches are globally oriented with regard to helping those in need, yet are unaware of people in their own congregations who need help. There are lots of ways you can help those in your own church:

- visiting shut-ins or those who are ill
- providing a ride for someone who is handicapped or unable to drive
- inviting someone single or recently divorced along for a family outing
- volunteering to repair, paint, or clean the house of an elderly, poor, or disabled person who cannot do these things on their own
- making cookies or a gift for someone new to the church
- writing your pastor a note of appreciation for his work
- committing yourself to some new area of weekly service
- praying with people who are in need

Serving those in your community. There are many opportunities to help others right in your own community. So many people are reluctant to give a homeless person money because they feel he or she might use the funds for cigarettes or alcohol. In my years of working with the homeless, I came to realize that many people living on the streets neither smoke nor are addicted to drugs or alcohol. But if you are concerned about giving money, offer to buy a sandwich for someone who is hungry. Or give them the blanket out of your car.

The list of social needs among people is almost endless. A few years ago I got involved with Prison Fellowship. Each time I go into a facility to teach a seminar, I am blessed by the inmates much more than they are by my words. Use the needs addressed by Jesus in the above Scripture to find your area of service—helping the hungry, the prisoner, the stranger, or any other of the least of these in your community.

Serving those in the world. Jesus commissions us to "go into the world and make disciples of all nations." Perhaps you have been able or will be able some day to travel to other lands so that they too might see the gospel revealed through your service. If this is not possible, perhaps you can provide financial gifts to those who do. Service to the world can be as easy as sending a letter to someone who is far from friends and family.

Learning to be actively involved in the spiritual disciplines is essential to our spiritual growth as Christians. My hope is that through daily prayer to the Father, continued study of the Scriptures, and service to others in the name of Christ, you may receive essential nourishment from the vine and bear the fruit God desires.

REFINING TIME COMMITMENTS

Bad habits can be broken. And new, healthy habits can take their place. When I began my journal many years ago, the daily entries did not come naturally. But with years of habit, ending my day with a journal entry is just as natural as turning off the light at night. If you do not actively participate in the spiritual disciplines, perhaps you need to create a plan by setting goals for your life.

The week before I started seminary, I spent five days of solitude in a mountain cabin some friends had graciously let me use. During that time I evaluated the lack of spiritual discipline in my own life. My first night there was the beginning of my journal. It was also a major turning point in my life.

As you begin to plan changes in your own life, I highly recommend a personal retreat away from all the hassles of life, as difficult as that may sound. I hope the following steps will be helpful as you develop your plan—whether you are able to get away for a week or merely a few hours.

Step One: Evaluate your current involvement in the disciplines. Before you actually develop a plan for changing your habits, use the table below to evaluate your current involvement in the spiritual disciplines discussed in this chapter. For each of the disciplines shown below, place a check mark next to the option that best describes the frequency of your involvement.

Current Participation in Spiritual Disciplines

Date: _____

Discipline	Daily	Weekly	Occasionally
Corporate prayer			
Private prayer			
Corporate worship			
Private devotional time			
Scripture study in a large group			
Scripture study in a small group			
Private Scripture study			
Journaling/Solitude with God			
Observing the Lord's Day			
Service to family and friends			
Service to my church			
Service to the community			
Service to the world			

Pay particular attention to those items you marked "occasionally" or those items you participate in weekly and would like to participate in daily. As you continue with your plan, decide which of these items are your top priorities.

Step Two: Evaluate your priorities with regard to time and set goals for change. Following is a list of activities that seem to take up the majority of our time. Two blank spaces have been provided for you to add other items that occupy your daily hours. (For example, writing might be an activity I would include here.)

Two columns have been provided to the right of the list of activities. In the first column rank each activity with regard to the priority you are currently giving it, "1" indicating the top priority. Try to think not only of the number of hours you spend on this activity, but also how important you are making it in your life. For instance, work may take up the majority of your time, but that doesn't make it your top priority. On the other hand, you cannot honestly put family time as a top priority if you are only spending fifteen minutes a week with your kids.

In the second column, labeled "goal," consider what priority you would like this activity to have in your daily life.

Time Priorities Evaluation

Activity	Current	Goal
Time at work		
Private devotional time		
Community devotional time		
Time with spouse		
Time with children		
Time with best friends		
Personal time (Rest)		
Time serving others		
_____		
_____		

Step Three: Making the time. In the exercise you just completed in Step Two, you compared the differences in your current or actual priorities to those priorities you would like to have. If your current priorities are different than those described as goals, you most likely will need to alter your schedule. You will want to spend less time on the items that are high on your current priority list but lower on your goal list. And you will want to spend more time on those items at the top of your goal list and low on your current priority list. Let's call those activities to which you'd like to give a higher priority the "goal activities."

Many of us are "yes" people. Even when our schedules are overbooked, we agree to provide some service for others who ask. As we've discussed in other chapters, even our commitment to church activities can become unhealthy if we lose our perspective on God or allow our personal relationships to deteriorate.

If your involvement in the spiritual disciplines has been affected because your schedule is so overwhelming, you may very well need to cut back in certain areas of your life to allow more time for your goal activities. If your priorities seem out of whack, practice saying the word "no" as often as you can. Next time someone asks you to become involved or volunteer for something new, get out your list of priorities and ask yourself, will this activity help me to become more involved in my goal activities?

Step Four: Set specific parameters for participating in spiritual disciplines. Hopefully, the spiritual disciplines ended up as high priorities among your goal activities. In developing your plan to become more involved in spiritual disciplines, consider how often you would like to do it and when and where you will do it. Use the table below to set up your own plan.

In the first column put a targeted starting date for the discipline to begin. If you are already participating regularly in an activity, write "ongoing" in this space.

In the second column write a time of day for practicing this discipline. Perhaps you will do your private prayer in the morning and journaling at night.

In the third column select a location where you plan to participate in each activity. Try to find a quiet, secluded place where you won't be distracted for your private devotions and prayer time.

Finally, set a goal for the frequency of each activity. If you plan on doing daily devotions, fill in the number "7." If you plan on attending church regularly each week but cannot make the Wednesday night service, put the number "1" in the row corresponding with corporate worship. When setting these and other goals, try to make sure they are realistic enough to attain, yet stretch you enough to encourage change.

Discipline	Date	Day	Location	Per Week
Corporate prayer	_____	_____	_____	_____
Private prayer	_____	_____	_____	_____
Corporate worship	_____	_____	_____	_____
Private devotional time	_____	_____	_____	_____
Scripture study in a large group	_____	_____	_____	_____
Scripture study in a small group	_____	_____	_____	_____
Private Scripture study	_____	_____	_____	_____
Journaling/Solitude with God	_____	_____	_____	_____
Observing the Lord's Day	_____	_____	_____	_____

Discipline	Date	Day	Location	Per Week
Service to family and friends	___	___	___	___
Service to my church	___	___	___	___
Service to the community	___	___	___	___
Service to the world	___	___	___	___

Step Five: Accountability. This is a most appropriate step to complete not only this chapter but the entire book. Regardless of which issues in this book you've chosen as goals for change, it will be important to your progress that you have either a small group or a special friend whom you can ask to help keep you accountable. Let this person or these people know what goals you have set for yourself and how you would like to change. Then set a time to meet regularly with your accountability person or team.

I have a friend whom I meet for lunch every week. It is the highlight of my week to share my struggles and successes with him and help him with his.

I wish to you, fellow Christians on a journey of change, growth, and new life in Christ, enough courage to break the bad habits, enough faith to survive the setbacks, and enough self-control to form new habits that heal. Remember as you enter the path through the narrow gate, when the ground gets rocky, when your footing becomes uncertain or when it seems to make more sense to turn back, God's grace will always be there to love you and accept you—just as you are. No one is a failure in God's eyes. Press on. Trade the habits that hurt you for new ones—habits that heal.

> Enter by the narrow gate; for the gate is wide, and the way is broad that leads to destruction, and many are those who enter by it. For the gate is small, and the way is narrow that leads to life, and few are those who find it. Mt 7:13-14

* NOTES *

* * *

INTRODUCTION
Lessons from a Stuck Friend

1. Milne, A.A., *Winnie-the-Pooh* (New York: E.P. Dutton, a Division of NAL Penguin, Inc., 1961), 26-33.

ONE
Can You Still See Me through the Clouds, God?

1. Marshall, Catherine, *Light in My Darkest Night* (Tarrytown, New York: Chosen Books, 1989), as excerpted by *Christian Herald*, September-October, 1989.
2. Marshall, Catherine, *Light in My Darkest Night*, as quoted in "Light in My Darkest Night," *Christian Herald*, September-October 1989, 26-28.
3. "The Face of God," *Life*, December, 1990, 47ff.

THREE
But I'm Not the One Who Blew It!

1. Shaver, Jessica, "Daughter of Manson Victims Finds Forgiveness," *Christianity Today*, September 22, 1989, 50ff.

SEVEN
I'll Start Tomorrow... If I Have the Time

1. Bonhoeffer, Dietrich, *Life Together* (New York: Harper and Row Publishers, 1954), 78.

Other Books of Interest
from Servant Publications

Changing on the Inside
Dr. John White

Changing on the Inside will convince readers that change for the better is not only possible but essential for their emotional and spiritual well-being. Dr. John White looks closely at the relationship between repentance and emotional health. He examines the nature of healthy and lasting change, resulting in peace, intimacy, and a vital connection with God.

This book explores the psychology and theology of change, guiding readers toward greater self-understanding. Dr. White uncovers the secret to making important life changes—how to open oneself to God's grace, find freedom from guilt, and experience profound and lasting recovery. *$8.99*

Healing Life's Hidden Addictions
Overcoming the Closet Compulsions that Waste Your Time and Control Your Life
Dr. Archibald Hart

Dr. Hart explores fascinating new research on addictive behaviors and the most effective way to overcome them. Co-dependency, perfectionism, denial, cravings, escape from boredom, the need for control, the avoidance of pain, and the pursuit of pleasure are just a few of the topics his book covers.

In addition to offering sound medical and psychological insight, Dr. Hart probes deeply into the spiritual dynamic at the heart of addiction and points to the path of grace that leads to healing. *$8.99*